D101966

Famous Gunfighters of the Western Frontier

Wyatt Earp, Doc Holliday, Luke Short and Others

W. B. (BAT) MASTERSON

DOVER PUBLICATIONS, INC.
MINEOLA, NEW YORK

Bibliographical Note

This Dover edition, first published in 2009, is an unabridged republication of the work originally published by *Human Life Magazine,* in 1907, and republished in book form by The Frontier Press of Texas, Houston, in 1957.

The photographs in this edition are reprinted courtesy of the *Noah H. Rose Photograph Collection,* Western History Collections, University of Oklahoma Libraries.

Library of Congress Cataloging-in-Publication Data

Masterson, Bat, 1853–1921.
    Famous gunfighters of the Western frontier : Wyatt Earp, "Doc" Holliday, Luke Short, and others / W.B. (Bat Masterson).
       p. cm.
    Originally published: Houston : Frontier Press of Texas, 1957.
    ISBN-13: 978-0-486-47014-6 (pbk.)
    ISBN-10: 0-486-47014-8 (pbk.)
    1.   Outlaws—West (U.S.)—Biography 2. Peace officers—West (U.S.)—Biography. 3. Outlaws—West (U.S.)—Biography—Pictorial works. 4. Peace officers—West (U.S.)—Biography—Pictorial works. 5. Frontier and pioneer life—West (U.S.) 6. West (U.S.)—Biography. 7. West (U.S.) —Biography—Pictorial works.

F590.5 .M37 2009
978/.020922—B22

                                                        2008055832

Manufactured in the United States of America
Dover Publications, Inc., 31 East 2nd Street, Mineola, N.Y. 11501

CONTENTS

WILLIAM BARCLAY (BAT) MASTERSON

William Barclay (Bat) Masterson has been engaged by Human Life to write a series of articles on the great old time gun-players of the West. The sketch in this issue considers Ben Thompson, whose name is as well known in Texas, and almost as well regarded in Austin at least, as that of General Sam Houston or Deaf Smith. Mr. Masterson himself is singularly well equipped for the task at hand. He will, from month to month, give us biographical and personal articles on Doc Holliday, Wyatt Earp, Buffalo Bill, Wild Bill Hickok, Charlie Ford, who killed Jesse James, Frank James, Clay Allison, Luke Short, and others once foremost among this hard-riding, quick-shooting chivalry of the plains. These men were the personal friends of Mr. Masterson. They have slept in his blankets, cooked by his campfire. Mr. Masterson has himself witnessed stirring times, and stood for years a central and commanding figure in a dangerous day that has gone. His life on the plains began when he was seventeen years old. He has been a buffalo hunter, Indian trader, Indian fighter. He was scout for Miles under the great Ben Clarke—now interpreter at the Cheyenne Agency—in the Indian war of 1874. He was in the weeks' war at the 'Dobe Walls on the Canadian, when he and thirteen other buffalo hunters fought five hundred of the picked bucks of the Cheyenne, Comanche, Kiowa and Arrapaho tribes, beat them and killed over eighty of them. Later, at the age of twenty-two, Mr. Masterson was elected sheriff of Ford county, Kansas, with headquarters at Dodge City, making a territory three hundred miles east and west by almost as many north and south. Dodge in that day was reckoned the roughest camp on the border. It was the northern terminus of the Jones and Plummer Trail, over which the beef herds came up from Texas. With them the cowboys—full of life, vivacity, and fight. It took a sure, cool hand to keep the peace in Dodge. That Mr. Masterson did not succeed in doing so without a struggle is evidenced by the fact that in the desperate combats of the pistol which ensued, he was driven to kill variously Walker, Wagner, Kennedy, Updegraffe and King, every one of whom was a "bad man," and had a gun in hand when he fell. But that day is past and Mr. Masterson is no longer a queller of "bad men," but a resident of New York and a contributor of the press. Also he is a warm personal friend of President Theodore Roosevelt, who caused him to be named Deputy United States Marshal for the Southern District of New York. President Roosevelt, following his election, was for naming Mr. Masterson Marshal in the Indian Territory. The place has twice the salary of the one he holds and carries with it the name of twenty-two deputies, and yet Mr. Masterson declined it. "It wouldn't do," he said. "The man of my peculiar reputation couldn't hold such a place without trouble. If I were to go out to the Indian Territory as Marshal, I can see what would happen. I'd have some drunken boy to kill once a year. Some kid who was born after I took my guns off would get drunk and look me over, and the longer he looked the less he'd be able to see where my reputation came from. In the end he'd crawl around to a gun play and I'd have to send him over the jump. Almost any other man could hold office and never see a moment's trouble. But I couldn't. My record would prove a never-failing bait to the dime novel reading youngsters, locoed to distinguish themselves and make a fire-eating reputation, and I'd have to bump 'em off. So, Mr. President, with all thanks to you, I believe I won't take the place. I've got finally out of that zone of fire and I hope never to go back to it." It was then that President Roosevelt did the next best thing, and caused Mr. Masterson's appointment as Deputy United States Marshal in New York.—Editor.

CHAPTER I

LUKE SHORT

The subject of this narrative might have "died with his boots on," for he had many chances—but he didn't. The fact that he lived to die in bed, with his boots removed, as all good folks like to do when the end has come, may have been due to good luck, but I hardly think so. That he was the quickest at the critical moment is, perhaps, the best answer.

When the time came for Luke Short to pass out of this life—to render up the ghost as it were—he was able to lie down in bed in a home that was his own, surrounded by wife and friends, and peacefully await the coming of the end.

There was nothing in his wan drawn features, as he lay on the last bed of sickness at Fort Worth, Texas, to indicate that luck had ever been his friend. He was aware that his time had come, and was reconciled to his fate. Every lineament in the cold, stern face, upon which death had already left its impress, showed defiance. He could almost be heard to say: "Death! You skulking coward! I know you are near; I also realize I cannot defeat you; but, if you will only make yourself visible for one brief moment, I will try!"

Was Known as a "White Indian"

Luke was a little fellow, so to speak, about five feet, six inches in height, and weighing in the neighborhood of one hundred and forty pounds. It was a small package, but one of great dynamic force. In this connection it will not be out of order for me to state that, though of small build, it required a 7⅛ hat to fit his well-shaped, round head. At the time he left his father's ranch in Western Texas, where he had been occupied as a cowboy in the middle seventies, for the Red Cloud Agency in North Dakota, he was nothing more than a white Indian. That is, he was an Indian in every respect except color. And as nearly all of our American Indians living west of the Missouri River in those days were both wild and hostile and on the war path most of the time, a fair idea of Luke Short may be gleaned from this statement. Luke had received none of the advantages of a school in his younger days; he could hardly write his name legibly. It was, indeed, doubtful if he had ever seen a school house until he reached man's estate. But he could ride a bronc and throw a lariat; he could shoot both fast and straight, and was not afraid.

He had no sooner reached the northern boundary line of Nebraska, hard by the Sioux Indian Reservation, than he established what he was pleased to call a "trading ranch."

His purpose was to trade with the Sioux Indians, whose reservation was just across the line in North Dakota. Instinctively he knew that the Indians loved whiskey, and as even in those days he carried on his shoulder something of a commercial head, he conceived the idea that a gallon of whiskey worth ninety cents was not a bad thing to trade an Indian for a buffalo robe worth ten dollars. Accordingly Luke proceeded to lay in a goodly supply of "Pine Top," the name by which the whiskey traded to the Indians in exchange for their robes was known.

Uncle Sam Objects to His Business

He was not long in building up a lucrative business; nor was it long before the Indian chiefs of the Sioux tribe got on to him. Drunken bands of young bucks were regularly returning to their villages from the direction of the

Short rendezvous loaded to the muzzle with "Pine Top," and, as every drink contained at least two fights and as it usually took about ten drinks to cause an Indian to forget that the Great White Father abode in Washington, the condition of those who had found entertainment at the Short ranch, when they reached their camp, can better be imagined than told.

The Indian agent in charge of this particular branch of the Sioux tribe with whom Short had been dealing soon got busy with Washington. He represented to the Department of the Interior that a band of cutthroat white men, under the leadership of Luke Short, were trading whiskey to his Indians, and that he was powerless to stop it, as the camp of the white men was located just across the reservation line, in the State of Nebraska, which was outside of his jurisdiction. He requested the government to instantly remove the whiskey traders and drive them from the country. Otherwise, said he, an Indian uprising will surely follow. The government, as was to be expected, forthwith instructed the post commander at Omaha to get after the purveyors of the poisonous "Pine Top," who were charged with causing such havoc among the noble red men of the Sioux reservation.

The military commander at Omaha soon had a company of United States cavalry after Short, and as he had no notice of such a move being made against him, he was soon a prisoner in the hands of the government authorities. He was alone in his little dugout, cooking his dinner, when the soldiers arrived. He was told that he was a prisoner, by order of the government, for having unlawfully traded whiskey to the Indians.

"Is that all, gentlemen?" said Luke, as he invited the officer in command of the soldiers to sit down and have a bite to eat with him.

"There will be no time for eating," said the officer, "as we must reach Sidney by tomorrow morning, in time to catch the Overland train for Omaha. So get together what things you care to take along, as we will be on our way."

"I have nothing that I care to take along," Luke replied, "Except what I have on;" and as that mostly consisted of a pair of Colt's pistols and a belt of cartridges, the officer soon had them in his custody.

"Where are your partners?" queried the Captain.

"I have no partners," replied Short. "I've been running this ranch by myself."

But Luke did have a partner, who was at that very time in Sidney procuring provisions and more "Pine Top."

After everything around the ranch resembling whiskey had been destroyed by order of the officer in command, the trip to Sidney, about seventy-five miles away, was taken up. Luke was put astride a government horse, his feet fastened with a rope underneath the animal's girth and told to ride in the center of the company of cavalrymen. Sidney was reached in time to catch the Overland train, and Luke was hustled aboard with as little ceremony as possible.

Luke had, by his quiet and diffident manner during the short time he had been prisoner, succeeded in having the officer regard him in the light of a harmless little adventurer, and for this reason did not have him either handcuffed or shackled, after placing him aboard the train for Omaha.

Sidney, Nebraska, was a very small place in those days. The permanent population in all probability did not exceed the one thousand mark. Sidney, following the custom of all small hamlets, however, would turn out when there was anything unusual going on. And the sight of a company of United States soldiers lined up at the railroad station was enough to arouse her curiosity and cause her townfolk to turn out in a body and investigate the cause. Luke Short's partner was among those who came to see the big show at the depot, and his surprise can well be imagined when he discovered that no less a person

than his partner wes responsible for the big event. It did
not take Luke and his partner long to fix up a code of
signals by which they could communicate with each other.
Luke could say a few things in Indian language that his
partner could understand, and to which he could make
comprehensible reply.

Short Escaped From the Soldiers

"Skidoo' and "Twenty-three" were terms familiar to
Short, even in those days. But they were conveyed by the
sign language instead of being spoken as now.

Luke made his partner understand that he would soon
be back in Sidney, and to have everything in readiness, so
that they could skip the country with as little delay as
possible, as soon as he showed up. The charge of having
unlawfully traded whiskey to the Indians did not seem
to concern him in the least. "I can beat that for sure,"
he said to himself; "But supposing that agent should take
a notion to call a count of heads. What then? I know that
there are several young bucks, whom I caught trying to
steal my 'Pine Top,' who will not be there to answer roll-
call, in case one is ordered. I planted those bucks myself,
and, outside of my partner, no one knows the location of
the cache. While I have no notion of putting in a claim
against the government for the work, I must be careful
and avoid having it endeavor to show that I really did
perform such service."

These were perhaps the thoughts he was conveying
by signals to his partner when he boarded the train at
Sidney that was to take him to Omaha.

To state the story briefly, Luke did not tarry long
with the soldiers after the train left Sidney. That night
found Luke back in town and before the following morning
both he and his partner were well on their way to Colorado,
driving a big span of mules hitched to a canvas-covered
wagon.

This happened in the fall of 1878 and, as Leadville

was just then having a big mining boom, Luke headed for Denver.

It must be remembered that in that country in those days there were no settlements of any kind, and by keeping from the line of the railroad, a white person was seldom seen.

A Little Affair In Leadville

Luke and his partner arrived in Denver in due course of time, and drove to one of the city horse corrals, where next day they disposed of their outfit at a good price. Luke's partner returned to his home in Austin, Texas, where his family connections were both wealthy and prominent. Luke went to Leadville, where everything was then on the boom. Here he began to associate with a class of people far different in manner, taste and dress from those he had been accustomed to. He was thrown in the society of rich mine buyers, as well as mining promoters. He got acquainted with gamblers and the keepers of the mining camp "honkatonks."

The whole thing was a new life to him, and he took to it like a duck to water. It was the first place where he saw the game of faro dealt, and he was fascinated. He was not long in camp before he was talked about. He ran foul of a bad man with a gun one day in one of the camp's prominent gambling houses, and the bad man, who had a record of having killed someone somewhere, attempted to take some sort of liberty with one of Luke's bets and, when the later politely requested the bad man to keep his hands off, the bad man became very angry and made some rude remarks. The dealer was frightened half out of his wits. He looked to see Short shot full of holes before anyone could raise a hand to prevent it. The dealer, of course didn't have Luke's number. He knew the other fellow, but had yet to become acquainted with the late vendor of "Pine Top" up Nebraska way.

"Gentlemen," said the dealer, in his most suave manner, "I will make the amount of the bet good, rather than have a quarrel."

"You will not make anything good to me," said Short. "That is my bet, and I will not permit anyone to take it."

"You insignificant little shrimp," growled the bad man, at the same time reaching for his cannister. "I will shoot your hand off, if you dare to put it on that bet."

But he didn't. Nor did he get his pistol out of his hip pocket. For, quicker than a flash, Luke had jammed his own pistol into the bad man's face and pulled the trigger, and the bad man rolled over on the floor. The bullet passed through his cheek but, luckily, did not kill him.

There was no arrest or trial. Such things happening all the time in those days in Leadville. This, however, gave Luke quite a standing. He was soon in big demand. Gambling-house proprietors wanted him to stay around their places of business during the busy hours, so as to keep the bad men in camp from carrying off their bank rolls. He had a faculty of making friends, and was soon popular with the quieter and better class of the sporting fraternity. He learned to play cards, and was soon dealing faro. No one who saw him then, togged out in tailor-made clothes and a derby hat, would have recognized in him the man who took the header from the Overland train ten miles east of Sidney, when he made the get-away from the soldiers.

Snuffing Out a Gambler

The spring of 1881 found Luke Short in Tombstone, Arizona, dealing faro in a house managed by Wyatt Earp.

One morning I went into the Oriental gambling house, where Luke was working, just in time to keep him from killing a gambler named Charlie Storms. There was scarcely any difference between this case and the one with the bad man in Leadville a couple of years previous. Charlie Storms was one of the best-known gamblers in the entire

West and had, on several occasions, successfully defended himself in pistol fights with Western "gun-fighters."

Charlie Storms and I were very close friends—as much as Short and I were—and for that reason I did not care to see him get into what I knew would be a very serious difficulty. Storms did not know Short, and, like the bad man in Leadville, had sized him up as an insignificant-looking fellow, whom he could slap in the face without expecting a return. Both men were about to pull their pistols when I jumped between them and grabbed Storms at the same time requesting Luke not to shoot, a request I knew he would respect if it was possible without endangering his own life too much. I had no trouble in getting Storms out of the house, as he knew me to be his friend. When Storms and I reached the street I advised him to go to his room and take a sleep, for I then learned for the first time that he had been up all night, and had been quarreling with other persons.

He asked me to accompany him to his room, which I did, and after seeing him safely in his apartment, where I supposed he could go to bed, I returned to where Short was. I was just explaining to Luke that Storms was a very decent sort of man when, lo and behold! there he stood before us. Without saying a word, at the same time pulling his pistol, a Colt's cut-off, 45 calibre, single action; but like the Leadvillian, he was too slow, although he succeeded in getting his pistol out. Luke stuck the muzzle of his pistol against Storms' heart and pulled the trigger. The bullet tore the heart asunder, and as he was falling, Luke shot him again. Storms was dead when he hit the ground. Luke was given a preliminary hearing before a magistrate and exonerated.

The Story of Two Rival Shows

In the spring of 1883 Luke formed a partnership with Harris and Beeson of Dodge City, and operated the Long Branch saloon, the biggest and best-paying gambling house in Dodge at the time. The mayor of Dodge, whose name was Webster, was also running a gambling house and saloon next door to that operated by Short. At this time Dodge City was the shipping point for the Texas cattle driven every summer from the great cattle ranges of Western Texas to the northern markets.

A fortune was to be made every season by the gambling house that could control this trade and, as Short was from Texas and had once been a cowboy himself, he held the whip-hand over the mayor, so far, at any rate, as the patronage of the cattlemen was concerned. This the mayor did not relish and, as he was a stubborn-minded man himself, who would brook no opposition if he could help it, he set to work to put Luke out of business. He had an ordinance passed by the City Council, prohibiting music in all the gambling houses and saloons in the city. Short employed a band in his place of business and Webster did likewise; but the latter was the mayor and therefore in control of the situation, so he thought. The city marshal was instructed by the mayor to notify Short that the music in his place must be discontinued.

"That suits me," Luke reported to have told the marshal. "I don't need music in my house in order to do business, and besides, maintaining a band is quite an item of expense."

The following night the only house in the city in which there was music was that operated by the mayor. Luke smelt a mouse then.

"We'll see about this," remarked Luke to his partners, Beeson and Harris.

The next night he re-engaged the band and instructed it to go ahead grinding out the old familiar melodies, so dear to the heart of the cowboy. Luke remained about the place for several hours to see what move, if any, was to be made by the mayor. As he saw nothing to cause alarm, he concluded to go away for a while and pay a visit to a sick friend. He had not left the place more than ten minutes before all the members of the band, among them one woman, the pianist, were arrested and locked up in the city calaboose.

Forced to Leave the Town

Luke was notified, and came hurriedly down to the saloon. He learned the facts of the arrest and went out to hunt up the officer who was in charge of the squad, in order that he might furnish bail for the musicians and have them released. But he could not find him or any other person who was considered competent to accept a bail bond. All the time Luke was trying to get his employees out of the calaboose, the music in the mayor's place was in full swing. This, as can well be imagined, did not tend to help matters in the least. About the time Luke had made up his mind that nothing could be done that night towards the release of the prisoners, he saw the officer whom he had been looking for standing some distance away. Luke started towards him.

The officer, who was standing on the sidewalk, which was a foot or so above the street, saw Luke coming, and instantly pulled his pistol and fired point blank at him. The shot missed and Luke returned the fire; but just as he pulled the trigger the officer started to run, and in leaving the sidewalk he fell. Luke, thinking he had hit him, went to his place of business, secured a shot gun and stood off the town until morning. He accomplished this by refusing to submit to arrest that night.

The next morning he was prevailed upon to lay aside his weapons, go over to the police court, plead guilty to creating a disturbance, pay a fine and have the whole thing ended. That was what had been promised him if he would take off his arms and surrender to the officers. He accordingly gave up his pistols and started for the police court, as they promised, they took him to the city jail and kept him locked up until the noon trains arrived. The passenger trains going East and West passed each other at Dodge, and Luke was marched to the depot by an escort armed with shotguns and told to choose which train he would take. There was nothing left for him to do. They had him, and were only waiting an excuse to riddle him with buckshot if he offered the least resistance.

He took the east-bound train and landed in Kansas City.

Lining Up for a Big Fight

I was in Denver at the time, and he wired me to come to Kansas City at once, which I did. We talked the matter over when we met, and concluded to go up to Topeka and place the matter before the Governor. The next day we did so. The Governor denounced the conduct of the Dodge City authorities, but said that he could do nothing, as the local authorities at Dodge had informed him that they were amply able to preserve the peace and did not desire state interference. We stated to the Governor that we believed we were able to rehabilitate ourselves in Dodge, but did not care to run afoul state authorities, in case we concluded to do so. The Governor told us to go ahead and re-establish ourselves, if we could; that he would keep off, and wished us luck. Immediately I started for Silverton, Colorado, where Wyatt Earp was located at the time, and enlisted him in our cause. Luke went to Caldwell, Kansas, where he had a couple of staunch friends, who were willing to take the bit in their mouths and go to the front and fight his battles whenever called upon. Inside of a week from the time forces were organized and were on the way to Dodge. It was decided that if a fight was all that would satisfy the mayor of Dodge,—a fight he would have.

Wyatt was selected to land in Dodge first. With him, but unknown to the Dodge authorities, were several desperate men. Several more dropped into town unobserved by the enemy. It finally became whispered about that Wyatt Earp had a strong force of desperate men already domiciled in town in the interest of Luke Short. The mayor called a hasty meeting of his friends and after they had all assembled in the council chamber of the city hall, informed them solemnly of what he had heard about the Earp invasion. Anyone who was present at that meeting could easily have seen that anything but a fight was what the mayor and his friends were looking for, not that such a thing was not altogether improbable. Someone present suggested that Wyatt be invited to attend the meeting and state, if he would, his position in the matter. The suggestion met with the instant approval of all present, and the mayor proceeded to forthwith appoint a committee to call upon Earp and inform him of its action. Wyatt was soon found, and told of the wishes of the assembled patriots.

A Conference With the Enemy

"It will afford me great pleasure to attend your meeting," was the laconic reply of the noble Warwick, and he was soon the central figure of as fine a collection of cutthroats as ever scuttled ship.

The mayor, addressing Wyatt, made inquiry as to the truth of the report that he and numerous other desperate men were in the city for the purpose of reinstating Short in Dodge.

"Mr. Mayor, and the gentlemen of the meetings," said Wyatt; "I guess the report is true. I came here some days ago," said he, "and, thinking that perhaps something might happen where I would need assistance, brought along some other gentlemen who signified a willingness to join in whatever festivities might arise."

"Moreover," continued Wyatt, "Luke and Bat will arrive at noon tomorrow, and on their arrival we expect to open up hostilities."

"Now, look here, Wyatt," said the mayor, "you have no better friends anywhere than we are, and we don't want any more fighting in this town. There has already been enough shooting and killing in Dodge to do for a while. Now, why can't this thing be fixed up before it goes any farther?"

"It can," said Wyatt, "If you are willing to allow Luke

to return and conduct his business unmolested as heretofore."

"I am perfectly willing to agree to that," said Webster. "And so are we," sung out the meeting in a chorus.

"All right, gentlemen," replied the phlegmatic Mr. Earp, "there shall be no conflict. I will proceed to inform both Mr. Short and Mr. Masterson of your decision in the case, and I will guarantee that if you keep your part of the agreement there shall be no bloodshed."

Wyatt immediately notified Short and I by wire of the complete backdown of the enemy, and when we reached the city next day we were cordially received by our friends. The enemy, not being sure that Wyatt could control the situation, kept in the background until he had received assurance from both Short and I that the peace terms made by Earp would be faithfully lived up to by us.

As soon as things quieted down a little, Short sent for the mayor and sheriff to meet him and some of his friends at his place of business for the purpose of talking over the situation and arriving at a better understanding. The mayor and sheriff came and with them the city attorney and the prosecuting attorney of the county. Short's party consisted of himself, his two partners, Beeson and Harris, Wyatt Earp and myself.

Luke addressed the mayor something after this fashion, after we had all settled down in our chairs:

"Mr. Webster, you have on the police force of this city two men who, without any reason known to me, showed themselves during the late trouble to be bitter enemies of mine. I want them removed from the force."

The mayor assured Luke that he need not give himself any further concern on that score, as both men complained of had already handed in their resignations and left town.

"Very well," said Luke. "There is, however, another thing I wish to call to your notice. You had an ordinance passed by the city council prohibiting music in saloons. I want that ordinance repealed."

"It shall be done," said the mayor, and turning to the city attorney, instructed him to prepare a call for a special meeting of the council to draw up an ordinance calling for the repeal of the objectionable one.

This ended Short's business with the mayor. He then turned to the sheriff and said in substance:

"Mr. Sheriff, you also have two men in your office that are objectionable to me and I would like to have you remove them." He then named the men, and the sheriff promised that they would have to go.

"Here are the names of the men you can appoint in their place," and he handed the sheriff a piece of paper containing the names of the men he desired appointed.

"All right, Luke," said the sheriff, "they are good enough for me."

Luke then turned around to the prosecuting attorney of the county and said, "I furnished bail for Mr. Blank in the sum of $2,000 before I was ordered to leave town, and I want that bail bond containing my name returned to me and all record of it destroyed."

"That will be easy," said the prosecutor.

"Now, gentlemen," said Luke "there being nothing further to do, suppose we return to the bar and take a little something just for old times' sake."

"All right," said everybody present, and the procession to the bar started.

Luke had won a bloodless battle, but that such was the case was no fault of his, for he had been willing to fight at any and all stages of the proceedings.

Short Owns The Town Again

We subsequently found that when Mayor Webster learned how he had been trapped by Earp, he hunted up the sheriff and prosecuting attorney and sent a hurry-up telegram to the Governor, which was signed by all three of them requesting him to send with as little delay as possible two companies of militia, assuring him that unless that was immediately done, a great tragedy would surely be enacted in the streets of Dodge City. The Governor, anticipating just such a move as this on the part of the authorities at Dodge as soon as they got frightened —and the telegram calling for the militia strongly indicated that that time had now arrived,—refused point blank to send the militia, and reminded the senders of the message that they had already repeatedly assured him that they were sufficiently able to handle the situation and did not need the militia; "and," said the Governor, in concluding his reply, "I expect you to do it."

When it became known in Dodge the sort of a reply the Governor had sent back to the appeal for militia, something of consternation took possession of the mayor's followers. Those who had lately been the loudest in their declarations of hostility to Short were now for peace at any price.

Webster, himself no coward, saw that the yellow streak he knew was in the makeup of his followers was giving unmistakable signs of recrudescence. He knew that when the time came he would have to fight the battle alone. He remembered that those very men upon whom he would now have to rely for support had already hid themselves from Short the night of the arrest of the musicians, and he could well imagine what they were likely to do now that Short had been strongly reinforced. It was at this stage of affairs that Webster concluded to send for Wyatt, and if possible bring a settlement of the difficulty without an appeal to arms. In making this move the mayor acted both wisely and timely; for had the case gone over to the next day there would have, in all probability, been bloodshed on both sides.

Luke, soon after his restoration to Dodge, concluded to settle up his affairs and move to Texas. He somehow could not bring himself to like those with whom he had so recently been on the outs, and that fall sold out all his interests in Kansas to his partners, and went to Texas.

The fall of 1884 found him the proprietor of the White Elephant gambling house in Fort Worth. The White Elephant was one of the largest and costliest establishments of its kind in the entire Southwest at the time. As a matter of course he made plenty of money, but it required a lot of money to keep him going, for he was one of the best-hearted men who ever lived. He could not say no to anyone, and, as might be expected, was continually being imposed upon by professional "cadgers," who make it a point to borrow all they can and never pay back anything. While he made fortunes in his gambling establishments, he died a comparatively poor man. He perhaps owed less and had more money due him when he died than any gambler who ever lived.

In the spring of 1887 I visited Short in Fort Worth and learned soon after my arrival that he was having some trouble which was likely to end seriously with a notorious local character by the name of Jim Courtright. It appears that this fellow Courtright, who had killed a couple of men in Fort Worth, also a couple more in New Mexico, and was therefore dreaded by almost the entire community, had asked Short to install him as a special officer in the White Elephant. Luke, who had been a substantial friend of Courtright's during his trouble at Fort Worth, told him he could not think of such a thing.

"Why Jim," said Luke, "I would rather pay you a good salary to stay away from my house entirely."

"You know," continued Luke, "that the people about here are all afraid of you, and your presence in my house as an officer would ruin my business."

Courtright, who was a sullen, ignorant bully, with no sense of right or wrong, could not see it as Luke did. He could not understand that it was a pure matter of business and would be much better for Short to hire him to stay away from the house altogether than to have him coming around it. At any rate Courtright got huffy at Luke and threatened to have him indicted and his place closed up. Courtright could not get it through his head how it was that Luke had dared to turn him down. He knew that he had everybody else in town "buffaloed" and could see no reason why Luke should be different from the others.

Luke and I were sitting together in the billiard room of the "White Elephant" one evening, discussing the trouble he was having with Courtright and the effect it was likely to have on his business.

Just then one of Luke's associates, by the name of Jake Johnson, came to where we were sitting and informed Luke that Courtright was in the outer lobby and would like to have a talk with him.

"Tell him to come in," said Short.

"I did invite him in," replied Johnson, "but he refused and said that I was to tell you to come out."

"Very well," said Luke, "I will see what he has to say"; and immediately got up and accompained Johnson to where Courtright was waiting.

It did not take Luke very long after meeting Courtright to discover that the latter's mission was anything but one of peace. He brought along no olive branch, but instead a brace of pistols, conspicuously displayed. It was not a parley that he came for, but fight, and his demeanor indicated a desire that hostilities open up forthwith.

No time was wasted in the exchange of words once the men faced each other. Both drew their pistols at the same time, but, as usual, Short's spoke first and a bullet from a Colt's 45-calibre pistol went crashing through Courtright's body. The shock caused him to reel backward; then he got another and still another, and by the time his lifeless form had reached the floor, Luke had succeeded in shooting him five times.

Luke was arrested on the spot by a deputy sheriff, and taken to the county jail, where he remained during the night. The next day he was taken before a justice of the peace, who held him for the grand jury in a normal bond. This ended the case, as the grand jury refused to indict on the evidence, holding that it was a case of justifiable homicide.

This ended Luke Short's shooting scrapes with the exception of a little gun dispute three years later at Fort Worth which had no fatal results.

I took occasion at the opening of this story to state that when Luke reached the age of young manhood he was totally lacking in education. It is now but proper for me to say that at the time of his death, twenty years later, he was an exceptionally wellread man. He could write an excellent letter; always used good English when talking and could quote Shakespeare, Byron, Goldsmith and Longfellow better and more accurately than most scholars.

To the burning of the midnight oil was due the transformation. It transformed him from a white Indian, when I first found him, to a diffident, courteous, gentleman, who was, at his death about twelve years ago, one of the best known and most popular sporting men in this country.

CHAPTER II

BEN THOMPSON

I have been asked by Human Life to write something about the noted killers of men I am supposed to have personally known in the early days on the western frontier and who of their number I regarded as the most courageous and the most expert with the pistol.

In making this request, I may reasonably assume the editor did not consider that he was imposing on me very much of a task, and had it embodied nothing more than the question of proficiency with the pistol, such would have been the case; but in asking me to offer an opinion on the question of physical courage as sometimes exemplified by them under nerve-trying conditions, he has placed a responsibility on my shoulders that I hardly care to assume. I have known so many courageous men in that vast territory lying west and southwest of the Missouri River—men who would when called upon face death with utter indifference as to consequences, that it would be manifestly unjust for me ever to attempt to draw a comparison.

Courage to step out and fight to the death with a pistol is but one of three qualities a man must possess in order to last very long in this hazardous business. A man may possess the greatest amount of courage possible and still be a pathetic failure as a "gun fighter," as men are often called in the West who have gained reputations as "man-killers." Courage is of little use to a man who essays to arbitrate a difference with the pistol if he is inexperienced in the use of the weapon he is going to use. Then again he may possess both courage and experience and still fail if he lacks deliberation.

Any man who does not possess courage, proficiency in the use of fire-arms, and deliberation had better make up his mind at the beginning to settle his personal differences in some other manner than by an appeal to the pistol. I have known men in the West whose courage could not be questioned and whose expertness with the pistol was simply marvelous, who fell easy victims before men who added deliberation to the other two qualities. I will cite a few such instances that came under my own personal observation.

The Harrison-Levy Feud

Thirty-five years ago Charlie Harrison was one of the best known sporting men west of the Missouri River. His home was in St. Louis but he traveled extensively throughout the West and was well known through the Rocky Mountain region. He was of an impetuous temperament, quick of action, of unquestioned courage and the most expert man I ever saw with a pistol. He could shoot faster and straighter when shooting at a target than any man I ever knew; then add to that the fact that no man possessed more courage than he did, the natural conclusion would be that he would be a most formidable foe to encounter in a pistol duel.

In 1876 he started for the Black Hills, which was then having a great mining boom on account of the discovery of gold at Deadwood. When Charley reached Cheyenne he became involved in a personal difficulty with another gambler by the name of Jim Levy, and both men started for their respective lodgings to get their pistols and have it out the first time they met. It looked like 100 to 1 that Harrison would win the fight because of his well known courage and proficiency in the use of the pistol. Little being known at that time about Jim Levy, Harrison was made a hot favorite in the betting in the various gambling resorts of Cheyenne. The men were not long in getting together after securing their revolvers, which were of Colt's pattern and of .45 calibre in size.

They met on opposite sides of the principal street of the city and opened fire on each other without a moment's delay. Harrison, as was expected, fairly set his pistol on fire, he was shooting so fast and managed to fire five shots at Levy before the latter could draw a bead on him. Levy finally let go a shot. It was all that was necessary. Harrison tumbled into the street in a dying condition and was soon afterwards laid to rest alongside of others who had gone before in a similar way.

That Harrison was as game a man as Levy could not be doubted; that he could shoot much faster, he had given ample proof, but under extraordinary conditions he had shown that he lacked deliberation and lost his life in consequence. The trouble with Charlie Harrison was just this— he was too anxious. He wanted to shoot too fast. Levy took his time. He looked through the sights on his pistol, which is a very essential thing to do when shooting at an adversary who is returning your fire.

Johnny Sherman, another well known Western sport

and a near relative of the famous Sherman family of Ohio, was another remarkably fine pistol shot. When he happened to be where he could go out and practice with his pistol, he would hunt up a shooting gallery and spend an hour or so practicing with the gallery pistols.

Wanted to Shoot Too Fast

In this way he became an adept in the use of the revolver. He was, as everyone who knew him can testify to, as courageous as a lion and yet, when he started in to kill a dentist in a room in a St. Louis hotel, who had, as he claimed, insulted his wife, he emptied his pistol at the dentist without as much as puncturing his clothes, and mind you, the dentist was not returning his fire. Sherman, like Harrison, was in too big a hurry to finish the job and forgot that there were a set of sights on his pistol.

Levie Richardson is another case in point that will serve to show that coolness and deliberation are very essential qualities in a shooting scrape, and unless a man possesses them, he is very apt to fall a victim to the man who does. Levie Richardson had been a buffalo hunter with me on the plains of western Kansas for several years. We were very close friends and shared our blankets with each other on a great many cold winter nights, when blankets were a very useful commodity. He was thoroughly familiar with the use of firearms and an excellent shot with either pistol or rifle. He was a high strung fellow who was not afraid of any man. He got a notion into his head one night in Dodge City, Kansas, that a young gambler by the name of Frank Loving, generally known as "Cock-eyed Frank," had done him some wrong, and forthwith made up his mind to kill him on sight. He publicly declared what he intended to do to Loving as soon as he met him, and some busybody who had been listening to the threats hastened away to put Loving on his guard.

Frank Loving was a mere boy at the time, but he was not afraid and immediately proceeded to arm himself and be prepared to deal out the best that he had when his man came. He did not have to wait very long, for Richardson was a man to act promptly when once he had made up his mind to do a certain thing; and as he had decided on killing Loving with as little delay as possible, the battle was on almost before a person had time to think. Richardson found Loving sitting unconcernedly on a card table in the Long Branch Saloon and instantly opened fire on him with his Colt's .45 calibre pistol. He fired five times at his man in rapid success, but missed with every shot and was finally shot dead by Loving who took his time about his work. It was the cleanest possible shot.

Richardson, like Harrison and Sherman, did not take sufficient time to see what he was doing, and his life paid the penalty. No one, however, who knew both men could truthfully say that Loving possessed a greater degree of courage than Richardson, or that under ordinary conditions he was a better marksman with a gun. Courage, generally speaking, is daring. Nerve is steadiness.

I was the sheriff of the county at the time and refused to lock Loving up in jail, holding that he had, in killing Richardson, only acted in self defense, and permitted him to be at large on his own recognizance until his preliminary examination was held, which exonerated him, as I knew it would. I have never stood for murder and never will, but I firmly believe that a man who kills another in defense of his own life should always be held blameless and will always lend a helping hand to such a man.

Frank Loving was himself murdered three years later by another gambler by the name of John Allen, in Trinidad, Colorado. Allen, soon after his acquittal for the murder of Loving, became a street preacher and of course all has been forgiven.

The Career of Ben Thompson

But all this is preliminary to the real purpose of this story, which is to tell something about Ben Thompson, the famous "gun fighter" of Austin, Texas. Ben Thompson was born in England and came to this country with his family when a boy. The family setttled in Austin, Texas, and Ben learned the printer's trade and set type in the local newspaper offices of the city.

When the Civil War broke out he enlisted as a private in one of the Texas regiments and went to the front to fight the battles of the lost cause. He was only a boy when he enlisted, but was not long in showing the kind of mettle that was in him. While serving in General Kirby Smith's command during the campaign along the Red River, young Thompson performed many deeds of great daring, such as crossing into the enemy's lines and in carrying important dispatches for the officers of his command. For the dash and courage he displayed at the battle of Sabine Cross Roads, just above the mouth of Red River in Louisiana, he was promoted to the rank of captain by his commanding officer. At the conclusion of hostilities between the North and South Ben returned to his home in Austin, but did not remain long. The spirit of war was now upon him and he longed for more conflict.

Austin was too peacefully disposed for him, so he immediately set out for old Mexico, where Maximilian was just then having a lively time maintaining himself in his position as Emperor of Mexico. After getting on Mexican soil Ben lost no time in reaching the headquarters of Maximilian's army, where he tendered his services in behalf of the invader's cause. He was instantly accepted and commissioned a captain and was soon wearing the uniform of the Emperor's army. Ben, however, was not given much opportunity to achieve distinction in the invading army, for Maximilian soon after suffered a collapse and Thompson was lucky to get away from the Mexicans and reach his home in Austin with his life.

Ben Thompson was a remarkable man in many ways and it is very doubtful if in his time there was another man living who equalled him with the pistol in a life and death struggle. Thompson in the first place possessed a much higher order of intelligence than the average "gun fighter" or man killer of his time.

He was more resourceful and a better general under trying conditions than any of that great army of desperate men who flourished on our frontier thirty years ago. He was absolutely without fear and his nerves were those of the finest steel. He shot at an adversary with the same precision and deliberation that he shot at a target. He was a past master in the use of the pistol and his aim was as true as his nerves were strong and steady. He had during his career more deadly encounters with the pistol than any man living and won out in every single instance. The very name of Ben Thompson was enough to cause the general run of "man killers," even those who had never seen him, to seek safety in instant flight. Thompson killed many men during his career, but always in an open and manly way. He scorned the man who was known to have committed murder, and looked with contempt on the man who sought for unfair advantages in a fight.

The men whom he shot and killed were without exception men who had tried to kill him; and an unarmed man or one who was known to be a non-combatant, was far safer in his company than he would be right here on Broadway at this time. He was what could be properly termed a thoroughly game man, and like all men of that sort never committed murder. He stood about five feet nine inches in height and weighed in later years in the neighborhood of 180 pounds.

Wore Silk Hat and Prince Albert

His face was pleasant to look upon and his head was round and well shaped. He was what could be called a handsome man. He was always neat in his dress but never loud, and wore little if any jewelry at any time. He was often seen on the streets of Austin, especially on a Sunday, wearing a silk hat and dressed in a Prince Albert suit of the finest material. While he was not given to taking any unnecessary chances with his life, he would unhesitatingly do so if he felt that occasion demanded it. For example:

He had a falling out one day with the proprietor of a vaudeville house in Austin and that night, just at the busiest hour, went over to the place and fired a shot from his pistol into one of the big chandeliers that was hanging from the ceiling, which broke some of the glass shades and scattered the pieces of broken glass in all directions over the audience. This, as might be expected, caused an immediate stampede of the patrons who rushed pell mell for the street. Thompson, when things quieted down somewhat, left the place without offering to do any further mischief. That seemed to satisfy Ben and in all probability the trouble would have ended then and there had the proprietor let the matter rest where it was; but he refused to listen to the advise of his friends and openly declared that he intended to get even with Thompson. As a matter of course everything he said about Ben was instantly carried to him and as is generally the way in such cases, some things he did not say were added to the story by the tale-bearers.

The Threat of the Vaudeville Man

At any rate it got noised about town that the vaudeville man was thoroughly organized for Ben and intended to kill him the first time he ever stepped inside his house. Of course Ben was told what was being said about him by the hurdy-gurdy manager, but only laughed and said that he guessed if he didn't die until he got killed by the showman, he would live a long time. But reports of the threats that were being made against his life by the vaudeville proprietor kept reaching him with such regularity, that he finally began to think that perhaps there might be something to them. At any rate he made up his mind to see for himself how much there really was in those threats that he had been hearing about for so long. So one night while the show was in full blast he told a very warm personal friend of his by the name of Zeno Hemphill that he had made up his mind to go over to the show and look over the arrangements he understood had been made for his removal from this vale of tears.

"Zeno," said Ben, "just fall in a few feet behind me and 'holler' if you see anything that doesn't look exactly right to you when I get inside that 'honkytonk.' Remember, Zeno, I only want you along for a witness in case anything happens," remarked Ben, as he started to cross the street to the variety theater that was soon to witness a terrible tragedy within its walls. Ben entered a door that led to the barroom from the street. This barroom was a part of the theater, although the stage upon which the performances appeared was in another part of the building.

In order to reach that part of the building in which a performance was being given it was necessary for Ben to pass along the entire length of the bar, then through a pair of swinging doors located about ten feet further on, through which it was necessary to pass before a view of the stage could be obtained. When Ben first entered the barroom he took a hasty survey of the surroundings but saw nothing to cause alarm. In fact he did not expect the attack to come from that part of the house, if indeed an attack was made at all, but was looking for it to occur after he had reached the theater proper, which would not be until after he had passed the swinging doors. Ben did not stop in the barroom but kept on walking leisurely towards the swinging doors, and just as he was about to push them apart he heard Zeno, who had just stepped into the room, cry out, "Look out, Ben." But before Ben could scarcely move, the bartender, whose name was Mark Wilson, had raised a double-barrelled shotgun that he had lying along the mixing board back of the bar, and emptied both barrels, which were heavily loaded with buckshot, at Ben, who could not have been more than ten feet away.

Incredible as it may seem Thompson escaped without a scratch. Mark Wilson, the bartender, was known to be a courageous young fellow who had on several occasions shown considerable fighting grit, and for that reason he had been selected to kill Thompson the first time he entered the place. Wilson, however, realizing that he was taking upon himself something of a job in agreeing to dispose of Ben Thompson, concluded that it would be best to get a little help, so he went to his friend Sam Mathews, and told him what he had made up his mind to do and asked him if he would help him out in the matter.

"With great pleasure," replied Mathews, and straightway went for his trusty Winchester rifle and immediately repaired to the variety theater to help out his friend Wilson in putting Ben Thompson out of the way.

When Ben entered the barroom that evening he saw Mathews standing around the corner of the bar, but did not notice that he had a Winchester rifle leaning by his side; in fact did not regard Mathews, whom he knew quite well, as an enemy and perhaps for that reason did not look him over very carefully. But to get to the point. The smoke from the shotgun had scarcely blown aside before Ben had whipped out his pistol and like a flash of lightning had shot Wilson dead in his tracks. Ben then noticed that Mathews had a Winchester rifle in his hand and instantly concluded that he too, was there for the purpose of aiding Wilson in killing him. Mathews seemed to anticipate what was passing through Thompson' mind, for he ducked down behind the bar instead of attempting to use the rifle. Thompson, instead of going around the end of the bar where he could see Mathews, took a rough guess at his location and fired through the end of the bar. The bullet struck Mathews squarely in the mouth and toppled him over on the floor.

When Case Was Called for Trial

Ben then turned around and walked out of the place with his friend, Zeno Hemphill, who later on, when the case was called for trial, was the most important witness for the defense. Ben was kept locked up in jail pending the preliminary examination and was then admitted to bail and subsequently acquitted.

This is only one of a dozen of such occurrences that could be cited in the career of this most remarkable man. Wilson and Mathews were unquestionable men of courage, else they could not have been induced to enter into a plot of killing such a desperate man as they knew Thompson to be; but when it came to the scratch they both lost their nerve and Ben was privileged to add two more names to the list of ambitious "gun fighters," who had sought to take his life. Thompson served a term as chief of police of the city of Austin and all the old-time citizens of the place remember him still as the best chief of police the city ever had. While Thompson was known throughout all that vast territory lying west and southwest of the Missouri River as the nerviest of men, and as unerring a shot with a pistol as ever lived; there were several men contemporaneous with himself who had the occasion arisen, would have given him battle to the death.

All With Nerves of Steel

Such men as "Wild Bill" Hickok, Wyatt Earp, Billy Tilghman, Charley Bassett, Luke Short, Clay Allison, Joe Lowe and Jim Curry were all men with nerves of steel who had often been put to the test—any one of whom would not have hesitated a moment to put up his life as the stake to be played for. Those men, all of them, lived and played their part and played it exceedingly well on the lurid edge of our Western frontier at the time Ben Thompson was playing his, and it is safe to assume that not one of them would have declined the gauge of battle with him had he flung it down to any one of their number.

In making this admission, however, I am constrained to say that little doubt exists in my mind that Thompson would have been returned the winner of the contest. Ben Thompson was murdered along with his personal friend, King Fisher, in a vaudeville theater in San Antonio, Texas, in March, 1884.

Both he and King Fisher were killed from ambush by a number of persons who were concealed in the wings of the stage, and neither ever knew what happened. Ben was hit eight times by bullets fired from a Winchester rifle, and King Fisher was hit five times. All the shots were fired simultaneously and both sank to the floor dead as it is possible to ever be. It was a cold-blooded, cruel and premeditated murder, for which no one was ever punished by law.

CHAPTER III

DOC HOLLIDAY

While he never did anything to entitle him to a statue in the Hall of Fame, Doc Holliday was nevertheless a most picturesque character on the western border in those days when the pistol instead of law determined issues. Holliday was a product of the state of Georgia, and a scion of a most respectable and prominent family. He graduated as a dentist from one of the medical colleges of his native state before he left it, but did not follow his profession very long after his diploma. It was perhaps too respectable a calling for him.

Holliday had a mean disposition and an ungovernable temper, and under the influence of liquor was a most dangerous man. In this respect he was very much like the big Missourian who had put in the day at the cross-road groggery and, after getting pretty well filled up with bug juice of the moonshine brand, concluded that it was about time for him to say something that would make an impression on his hearers; so he straightened up, threw out his chest and declared in a loud tone of voice, that he was "a bad man when he was drinking and managed to keep pretty full all the time." So it was with Holliday.

Physically, Doc Holliday was a weakling who could not

have whipped a healthy fifteen-year-old boy in a go-as-you-please fist fight, and no one knew this better than himself, and the knowledge of this fact was perhaps why he was so ready to resort to a weapon of some kind whenever he got himself into difficulty. He was hot-headed and impetuous and very much given to both drinking and quarrelling, and, among men who did not fear him, was very much disliked.

He possessed none of the qualities of leadership such as those that distinguished such men as H. P. Myton, Wyatt Earp, Billy Tilghman, and other famous western characters. Holliday seemed to be absolutely unable to keep out of trouble for any great length of time. He would no sooner be out of one scrape before he was in another, and the strange part of it is he was more often in the right than in the wrong, which has rarely ever been the case with a man who is continually getting himself into trouble.

The indiscriminate killing of some negroes in the little Georgia village in which he lived was what first caused him to leave his home. The trouble came about in rather an unexpected manner one Sunday afternoon—unexpected so far at least as the negroes were concerned. Near the little town in which Holliday was raised, there flowed a small river in which the white boys of the village, as well as the black ones, used to go in swimming together. The white boys finally decided that the negroes would have to find a swimming place elsewhere, and notified them to that effect. The negro boys were informed that in the future they would have to go further down the stream to do their swimming, which they promptly refused to do and told the whites that if they didn't like existing conditions, that they themselves would have to hunt up a new swimming hole.

As might have been expected in those days in the South, the defiant attitude taken by the negroes in the matter caused the white boys to instantly go upon the war path. They would have their order obeyed or know the reason why. One beautiful Sunday afternoon, while an unusually large number of negroes were in swimming at the point of dispute, Holliday appeared on the river bank with a double-barrelled shot-gun in his hands, and, pointing it in the direction of the swimmers, ordered them from the river.

"Get out, and be quick about it," was his preemptory command. The negroes, as a matter of course, stampeded for the opposite shore, falling over each other in their effort to get beyond the range of the shot-gun. Holliday waited until he got a bunch of them together, and then turned loose with both barrels, killing two outright, and wounding several others.

The shooting, as a matter of course, was entirely unjustifiable, as the negroes were on the run when killed; but the authorities evidently thought otherwise, for nothing was ever done about the matter. Holliday, afterwards in speaking about the occurrence, justified the deed on the broad grounds that the "niggers" had to be disciplined, and he knew of no more effective way of doing it than with a shotgun. His family, however, thought it would be best for him to go away for a while and allow the thing to die out; so he accordingly pulled up stakes and went to Dallas, Texas, where he hung out his professional sign bearing the inscription, "J. H. Holliday, Dentist." This was in the early seventies and at the time when Dallas was a typical frontier town in everything the term implied. A stranger in Dallas in those days could get anything he wanted from pitch and toss to manslaughter at any hour of the day or night, and that was exactly what suited the Georgia dentist.

Gambling was not only the principal and best-paying industry of the town at the time, but it was also reckoned among its most respectable and, as the hectic Georgian had always shown a fondness for all things in which the elements of chance played an important part, his new environment furnished him with no cause for complaint. In a short time those who wished to consult professionally with the doctor, had to do so over a card table in some nearby gambling establishment, or not at all. While Holliday never boasted about the killing of the negroes down in Georgia,

he was nevertheless regarded by his new-made Texas ac-
quaintances who knew about the occurence, as a man with
a record; and a man with a record of having killed someone
in those day, even though the victim was only a "nigger,"
was looked upon as something more than the ordinary mor-
tal; wherefore the doctor on that account was given instant
recognition by the higher circles of society in Dallas.

If there was any one thing above another Holliday
loved better than a session in a poker game, it was conflict,
and, as Dallas was the home of conflict, the doctor was in
his element. It was not a "nigger" that he shot this time,
but a white man of some local prominence for which he had
to emigrate to some more congenial place. He brought up
next at Jacksboro, a small, out-of-the way place just off the
Fort Richardson Military Reservation, on the northwestern
border of the state, where civilization was only in a forma-
tive stage.

The doctor had by this time heard much about the man-
killers who abode on the frontier, and regarded himself as
well qualified to play a hand among the foremost of the
guild. He was not long in Jacksboro before he was in another scrape. This time it was with a soldier who was sta-
tioned at the fort, who had been given permission to visit
the town by his commanding officer. The trouble was over
a card game in which the soldier claimed he had been given
the worst of it by the man from Georgia. This of course,
necessitated the fighting Georgian taking another trip on
the road, for he knew it would never do to let the soldiers at
the fort capture him, which they would be sure to try to
do as soon as word reached them about the killing of their
comrade. He therefore lost no time in getting out of town,
and seated on the hurricane deck of a Texas cayuse, was
well on his way to safety by the time the news of the homicide reached the fort. It was a long and dangerous trip that
he mapped out for himself on this occasion.

From Jacksboro to Denver, Colorado, was fully eight
hundred miles, and as much of the route to be traversed

through was the Texas Panhandle, and No Man's Land, which in those days was alive with Indians none too friendly to the white man, and renegade Mexicans from New Mexico, the journey was a most perilous one to take; but the doughty doctor was equal to the task and in due time reached Denver without either having lost his scalp, or his desire for more conflict. This was in the summer of 1876 and while Denver was a much more important city than Dallas, its local government was conducted on very much the same principles. Like Dallas, everything went in Denver, and the doctor, after looking the situation over for a day or two, concluded that he had lost nothing by the change.

In all respects the Rocky Mountain town looked good to him, and as he had set out to build up a record for himself as a man-killer, he did not purpose lying idle very long. While Denver, in many respects in those days was a rough and ready town, it nevertheless enforced to the very letter the ordinance against the carrying of fire arms, and Holliday, for the nonce becoming prudent, put his cannister aside, but straightway went and bought himself a murderous looking knife. Thus heeled, he did not long delay in getting into action, and in so doing, carved up the face and neck of one Bud Ryan, a quiet and gentlemanly looking sport, in a frightful manner. Bud Ryan still lives in Denver, and carries around with him marks of his run-in with the fighting Holliday more than thirty years ago. It was again the doctor's turn to take the road and escape from the scene of his recent malefaction, and this time he headed for Dodge City, Kansas. It was there I first met him, although I had heard about his doings in Texas.

He was slim of build and sallow of complexion, standing about five feet ten inches, and weighing no more than 130 pounds. His eyes were of a pale blue and his moustache was thin and of a sandy hue. Dodge City was then very much like Dallas and Denver, only a little more so, and the doctor did not express regret at having come. It was easily seen that he was not a healthy man for he not only looked the part, but he incessantly coughed it as well. During his year's stay at Dodge at that time, he did not have a quarrel with anyone, and, although regarded as a sort of grouch, he was not disliked by those with whom he had become acquainted. It was during this time that he also made the acquaintance of Wyatt Earp and they were always fast friends ever afterwards.

He went from Dodge to Trinidad, Colorado, where, within a week from the time he landed, he shot and seriously wounded a young sport by the name of Kid Colton, over a very trivial matter. He was again forced to hunt the tall timber and managed to make his escape to Las Vegas, New Mexico, which was then something of a boom town, on account of the Santa Fe Railroad having just reached there. Holliday remained around Las Vegas for some time, doing the best he could in a gambling way; then he had a quarrel with one of the town rounders by the name of Mike Gordon, whom he invited to step outside of the saloon in which they were quarrelling. No sooner had Gordon stepped from the door than Holliday shot him dead. From Las Vegas to Dodge City across country, without following the traveled road, was about five hundred miles, and this was the trip Holliday was again compelled to make on horseback, in order to get away from the authorities who were hot on his trail. He reached Dodge City safely and remained there until Wyatt Earp took him in his covered wagon to Arizona in the fall of 1880. Again he showed no disposition to quarrel or shoot while in Dodge, and many thought that much of the trouble he had been having in other places had been forced upon him, but I am satisfied that it was pretty much all of his own seeking. His whole heart and soul were wrapped up in Wyatt Earp and he was always ready to stake his life in defense of any cause in which Wyatt was interested. He aided the Earp brothers in their street fight in Tombstone, against the Clanton and McLowery brothers, in which the latter two were killed, along with Billy Clanton.

It was Doc Holliday, who, along with Wyatt Earp, overtook and killed Frank Stillwell at the railroad station in Tucson for having participated in the murder of Morgan Earp in Tombstone. He was by Wyatt's side when he killed Curly Bill at the Whetstone Springs outside of Tombstone. Damon did no more for Pythias that Holliday did for Wyatt Earp.

After Wyatt and his partner had run down and killed nearly all their enemies in Arizona, Holliday returned to Denver, where he was arrested on an order from the Arizona authorities, charged with aiding in the killing of Frank Stillwell. This happened in the spring of 1882. I was in Denver at the time, and managed to secure an audience with Governor Pitkin who, after listening to my statement in the matter, refused to honor the Arizona requisition for Holliday. I then had a complaint sworn out against Holliday, charging him with having committed a highway robbery in Pueblo, Colorado, and had him taken from Denver to Pueblo, where he was put under a nominal bond and released from custody. The charge of highway robbery made against Holliday, at this time, was nothing more than a subterfuge on my part to prevent him from being taken out of the state by the Arizona authorities, after Governor Pitkin went out of office, but the Colorado authorities did not know it at the time. Holliday always managed to have his case put off whenever it would come up for trial, and by furnishing a new bond, in every instance would be released again.

When he died at Glenwood Springs a few years afterwards, he was still under bond to answer to the charge of highway robbery I had caused a certain person to prefer against him. Doc Holliday, whose right name was John H. Holliday, lived during his stormy career in three states of the Union besides the one in which he was born, and in two territories; namely Texas, Colorado, and Kansas, and in the territories of New Mexico and Arizona. Besides the killing of the negroes in the river in his home town, he shot a man in Dallas, Texas, and killed another in Jacksboro. He stabbed Bud Ryan in a frightful manner in Denver, Colorado, and shot another in Trinidad in the same state. He killed a man in Las Vegas, New Mexico, and was directly connected with several killings in Arizona.

Kansas, it will be observed, was only the state in which he lived in which he failed to either slay or bodily wound some person. The question as to the extent in which he was justified in doing as he did, is of course open to debate. I have always believed that much of Holiday's trouble was caused by drink and for that reason held him to blame in many instances. While I assisted him substantially on several occasions, it was not because I liked him any too well, but on account of my friendship for Wyatt Earp, who did.

Holliday had few real friends anywhere in the West. He was selfish and had a perverse nature—traits not calculated to make a man more popular in the early days on the frontier.

CHAPTER IV

BILL TILGHMAN

Nothwithstanding the discovery of gold in California in 1849, and at Pike's Peak, Colorado, ten years later, the civilizing of the West did not really commence until after the close of the Civil War. It was during the decade immediately following the ending of the conflict between the North and South that civilization west of the Missouri River first began to assume substantial form.

It was during this period that three great transcontinental lines of railroads were built, all of them starting at some point on the west bank of the Missouri River. The Union Pacific from Omaha to Ogden, Utah, was completed during these years, also the Kansas Pacific, from Kansas City to Denver, Colorado, and the Atchison, Topeka and Santa Fe from Atchison, Kansas, to Pueblo, Colorado. In twenty years from the day the first railroad tie was laid on the roadbed of the Union Pacific at Omaha, our Western frontier had almost entirely disappeared. There has been no frontier in this country for a good many years. The railroads long ago did away with all there ever was of it. Railroad trains, with their Pullman cars and dining car connections, have been reaching almost every point in the West of any consequence for the last twenty years.

On what was once known as our great American plains, which, a generation ago, furnished a habitat for the wild Indian, the buffalo, the deer and the antelope, today can be seen thousands of beautiful homes, in which none of the evidences of higher civilization are lacking. While it required but twenty years or so to bring about this wonderful change in this vast territory, the task was by no means an easy one.

Let the reader remember that in those twenty years, no less than half a dozen bloody Indian wars were fought, and that the scenes of these conflicts extended from the Dakotas on the north to the lava beds of Oregon on the west, and south to the frontier of Texas; and a fairly good idea of the magnitude of the undertaking will be gained. It was during those stirring times that nearly all of the famous characters of our once immense frontier, many of whom are now but memories, played a conspicuous part in this vast theater of human strife.

James B. Hickok (Wild Bill) was perhaps the only one of that chivalrous band of fighting men, who composed the vanguard of western civilization, who had acquired fame before the period I have named. When this most remarkable man came to the West at the close of the Civil War, in which he had taken a conspicuous part both in Southwest Missouri and in the campaign along the Mississippi River, he brought with him a well-earned reputation for daring and physical courage—a reputation he successfully held until stricken down by the Assassin Mc-Call at Deadwood, in June, 1876. But it was not of Wild Bill I started to write, but of one whose daring exploits on the frontier will not suffer by comparison.

The purpose of this article is to tell the story of Bill Tilghman, who was among the first white men to locate a buffalo hunting camp on the extreme southwestern border of Barbour County, Kansas, just across the Indian Reservation line, as far back as 1870. Bill Tilghman is one of the few surviving white men who reached the southwest border of Kansas before the advent of railroads, who is still in harness and to all intents and purposes as good both physically and mentally as ever.

It is now thirty-seven years since a slim-built, bright-looking youth, scarcely seventeen years old, pulled up for camp one evening on the bank of the Medicine Lodge River in Southwestern Kansas, only a few miles north of the boundary line between Kansas and the Indian Territory. An Indian uprising lasting more than a year had been put down the year previous by General Custer, and, as a natural consequence, the Indians who had taken part in the uprising entertained for the white man anything but a friendly feeling.

Billy Tilghman, like the others in that country at the time, became a buffalo hunter and was working along nicely until the Indians got after him. The Indians, by the terms of the treaty lately concluded with the government, had no right to leave their reservation without first obtaining permission from their agent. It was therefore as unlawful for an Indian to be found in Kansas without government permission, as it would have been for a white man to enter the Indian Territory for the purpose of either hunting or trading whiskey with the Indians. The Indians, however, cared little for treaty stipulations at the time and often crossed over into Kansas for the purpose of pillage as well as killing buffalo.

The Indian, besides destroying the hunter's buffalo hides and carrying away his provisions and blankets while be was temporarily away attending to the day's hunting on the range, was often known to have added murder to his numerous other crimes, so that an Indian off his reservation got to be viewed with apprehension by the hunters. It was a well understood thing among the buffalo hunters whose camps were located close to the reservation line, that any time a hunter could be taken unawares by the Indians he was almost sure to be killed, if for no other reason than to secure his gun and belt of cartridges. The Indians had, in prowling around the country one day come upon Billy Tilghman's camp, and, after cutting up what hides he had staked out on the ground for drying purposes, proceeded to set fire to those already dried and piled up ready for market.

When Tilghman and his two companions returned to camp that evening, after their day's work on the range, they found their camp a complete wreck. Besides the destruction of several hundred dollars' worth of hides, they also found that the noble red men who had paid their camp a visit during their absence had carried off everything there was to eat. But, as buffalo hunters found no trouble in making a hearty meal of buffalo meat alone, they did not despair nor go to bed on an empty stomach.

The day's hunt had resulted in the taking of twenty-five buffalo hides, and the question now arose what was to be done with them. If they were staked out to dry as the others had been, there was no reason for believing the Indians would not return and destroy them as they had the others. Tilghman's two partners were for moving away the first thing in the morning.

"We are liable to all be killed," said one of them, "if we stay here any longer."

"I think we ought to go about twenty miles farther north over on Mule Creek," said the other. "Besides the hunting is as good there as it is here, and the Indians hardly ever get that far away from the reservation."

"We will move away from here," said Billy Tilghman in his characteristically deliberate manner, "after I get even with those red thieves for the damage they have done us."

Billy Tilghman, although a mere boy at the time, was the master-mind of that camp, and what he said was law.

"Ed," said Billy to one of the partners, "go and hitch up the team and drive to Griffin's ranch and get a sack of flour, some coffee and sugar and a sack of grain for the horses and get back here before daylight in the morning, and Henry and I will unload those hides and peg them out to dry. Don't forget to feed the team when you get there and let them rest up for an hour or two, as you will have plenty of time to do that and get back here by day-break."

Griffin's ranch was fifteen miles north of Tilghman's camp on the Medicine Lodge River and the only place near-er than Wichita, which was one hundred and fifty miles farther east, where hunting supplies and provisions could be obtained.

Ed was soon on his way to Griffin's ranch, which only took three hours to reach. While Tilghman and Henry were busily engaged in fleshing and staking out the green hides, Billy remarked that if those thieving Cheynnes came again around his camp for the purpose of destroying things, there would likely be a big pow-wow take place among the Indians as soon as the news of what occurred reached them, "For," said he with some emphasis, "I don't intend to stop shooting as long as there is one of them in sight."

"But supposing," said Henry, "that there is a dozen or so of them when they come, what then?"

"Kill the entire outfit," replied Billy, "if they don't run away."

There was little else said on the subject before bed-time, but as Henry afterwards told me, it was a hard mat-ter to understand by Tilghman's actions that the only thing that seemed to worry him was the fear that the Indians would fail to pay the camp another visit.

Before daylight the following morning Ed was back in camp, having carried out his instructions to the letter. After breakfast that morning, Tilghman informed Ed and Henry that they would have to hunt without him that day, as he intended to conceal himself near the camp, so as to be in a position to extend a cordial welcome to the pillaging red-skins when they showed up. Billy as a precaution, planted himself before the other boys left for the hunting ground, so that in case the camp was being watched by the Indians, they could not tell but what they had all left camp as they had done the previous day. About noon, and just as Billy was commencing to despair, one lone Indian made his appearance. He rode up very leisurely to the top of a little knoll where he could get a good view of the camp, and, after a careful survey of the surroundings, and discovering nothing to cause alarm, proceeded to make the usual Indian signals, which is done by circling the pony around in different ways. Tilghman, who was crouched down in his little cache, was intently watching the Indian, understanding as well as the redskin did, the meaning of the pony's gyrations. Directly six other Indianc rode up alongside of the first and proceeded to carefully make a mental note of everything in sight.

They soon concluded that there was no lurking danger and all rode down to the camp and dismounted. This was exactly what Billy had been hoping they would finally conclude to do. Now if they will only all dismount, said Billy to himself, as he saw the Indians riding down to camp, I will kill the last one in the outfit before they can remount. He got his wish, for they all hopped off as soon as camp was reached. Billy, however, waited for awhile to see if they intended mischief, before opening up on them with his Sharp's big fifty buffalo gun that burned 120 grains of powder every time it exploded a shell. He did not have long to wait, for no sooner had one big buck hit the ground than he ran over to the sack of flour and picked it up and threw it across his pony's back, while some of the others started out, as Billy supposed, to cut up the freshly staked hides.

The big Indian who had swiped the sack of flour had scarcely turned around before Tilghman dropped him in his tracks with his rifle. This, as might be supposed, caused a panic among the other Indians, who little suspected that there was an enemy nearer than the hunting ground, until they heard the crack of the gun. In an instant Billy had in another cartridge, and another thieving Cheyenne was sent to the happy hunting grounds. The first Indian that succeeded in reaching his pony had no sooner mounted him than he was knocked off by another bullet from Billy's big fifty. This made three out of the original seven already killed, and what was an unusual thing for a Southern Plains Indian to do, the remaining four abandoned their ponies and took it on the run for a nearby clump of timber, which all but one reached in safety. Billy managed to nail one more of the fleeing marauders before he could reach the sheltering protection of the woods. The shooting attracted the attention of his partners, who were not more than two miles away, causing them to hurry to camp, where they expected to have to take a hand in a fight with Indians, whom they had reason to believe were responsible for the shooting they had heard.

"The scrap is over," said Billy, when the boys got near enough to hear him, "and three of the hounds have made their escape. I told you last night, didn't I Henry, that I would kill all that came if they stood their ground and didn't run away. Well," he said in a rather disconsolate tone of voice, "I fell down somewhat on my calculations, as seven came and I only succeeded in getting four, but then that wasn't so bad, considering that they left us their ponies."

"What's to be done now?" inquired Henry, who was not hankering for a run in with the Indians at that time.

"Don't get frightened," said Billy; "and remember that we are in Kansas and that those dead Indians were nothing more than thieving outlaws who had no right off their reservation and if any more of them come around before we are ready to leave, we will start right in killing them."

There was nevertheless little time wasted in getting away from that locality. The camp dunnage was loaded into the wagon in a hurry, and the team headed towards the north, and Ed, who was driving, was told to keep up a lively trot whenever possible. Billy brought up the rear mounted on one of the Indian ponies and driving the others.

"Look here, Billy," said Henry, as they were about to pull out of camp, "don't you think we ought to bury those dead Indians before leaving?"

"Never mind those dead Indians," replied Tilghman, "The buzzards will attend to their funeral; go ahead."

When dark overtook the party that night they were on Mule Creek, twenty-five miles from where they had pulled up camp at noon. The Indians reported the occurrence of the killing to their agent at the Cheyenne Agency, but received no satisfaction, and were informed that they were liable to be killed every time they left their reservation without permission.

That was Tilghman's first mix-up with the Indians but it was not his last. He continued to hunt in that country, and as the Indians persisted in crossing over into Kansas, there were many clashes between them, with invariably resulted in the Indians getting the worst of the encounter.

A Scout for the Government

During the fall and winter of 1873-4, there was practically no cessation of hostilities between the Indians and hunters along the Indian border, finally culminating in an uprising among the four big Southern tribes, namely the Cheyennes, Arapahoes, Kiowas and Comanches, which required almost a year for the government to put down. In this Indian war of 1874, Tilghman acted as a scout for the government and several times while carrying dispatches from one commander to another had to fight his way out of mighty tight places with the Indians in order to save himself from being taken alive. After the Indian uprising had been put down, Tilghman went up on the Arkansas River and took up a ranch close to Dodge City, where he lived for several years. In 1884 he was appointed City Marshal of Dodge City, and made one of the most efficient marshals the city ever had. He was just the sort of a man to run a town such as Dodge City was in those days, being coolheaded, courageous and possessing excellent executive ability.

In the summer of 1888, a county seat war broke out in one of the northern tier of counties in the state of Kansas, and Tilghman was sent for by one of the interested parties to come up there and try and straighten the matter out. Tilghman went and took with him a young fellow by the name of Ed Prather, whom he had every reason to believe he could rely upon in case of an emergency. Prather, however, proved to be a traitor, and one day attempted to assassinate Tilghman, but the latter was too quick for him, and Prather was buried the next day. After straightening out the county seat trouble, Billy returned to Dodge and continued to live there until the opening up of the Oklahoma territory, fifteen years ago.

He was among the first to reach the Territory, and took up a claim at Chandler, Lincoln County, where he still resides. Tilghman acted as U. S. Deputy Marshal when he first went to Oklahoma and did as much if not more to stamp out outlawry in the Territory as any other man who ever held office in that country.

The Capture of Bill Doolin

Tilghman has served four years as Sheriff of Lincoln County, and during that time has killed, captured and driven from the country a greater number of criminals than any other official in Oklahoma or the Indian Territory. His capture of Bill Doolin in a bath house at Eureka Springs, Arkansas, single handed, was perhaps the nerviest act of his official career. Doolin was known to be the most desperate criminal ever domiciled in the Indian Territory and had succeeded for several years in eluding capture. A large reward was offered for his apprehension and a number of U. S. Marshals with their deputies had several times attempted to arrest him, dead or alive, but in every instance Doolin either eluded them or, when too closely pressed, stood them off with his Winchester. Doolin was credited with the killing of several Deputy Marshals. Tilghman got after him and trailed him to Eureka Springs where he found him in a bath house, and without calling on the local officials for assistance, effected his capture single-handed. Doolin was seated on a lounge in the bath house when Tilghman entered, and before the desperado realized what was happening, he was covered by a 45-calibre Colt's pistol and ordered to throw up his hands. Doolin hesitated about obeying the order and Tilghman was forced to walk right up to him and threaten to shoot his head off unless he instantly surrendered. Doolin had his pistol inside his vest and directly under his armpit, and made several attempts to get it before he was finally disarmed. It was certainly a daring piece of work on the part of Tilghman, and he was lucky to get away with the job without being killed.

Bill Raidler was another notorious outlaw whom Tilghman got after, but in this case the Marshal was forced to kill his man before he could take him. Tilghman and Raidler met in the road in the Osage Indian country, and Tilghman ordered the outlaw to throw up his hands, but instead of obeying he opened fire on the Marshal, who instantly poured a fistful of buckshot into the desperado's breast, killing him in his tracks. Raidler had been a pal of Doolin's and had been mixed up in several train robberies and had sent word to the U. S. Marshals that if they wanted him to come and get him, but to be sure and come shooting. Tilghman was too good a shot for him at the critical moment and Bill Raidler's life paid the penalty for his many crimes.

Thomas Calhoun, a negro, was another outlaw and

murderer whom Marshal Tilghman captured in the Territory, but not until after he had shot and broken the desperado's leg did he succeed in making him a prisoner. Calhoun was charged with the murder of a colored woman and a warrant for his arrest placed in Marshal Tilghman's hands. The Marshal came upon Calhoun and ordered him to throw up his hands, which he refused to do, and promptly opened fired on Tilghman, who as he had so often done before, returned it with such good effect that the negro's leg was broken and he then surrendered, but died soon afterwards.

Dick West, known as "Little Dick," was perhaps the worst criminal in the entire territory, outside of Bill Doolin. "Little Dick" was a member of the Doolin gang of train robbers, and the hardest outlaw in the Territory to trap. He never slept in the house, winter or summer, and kept continually changing from one place to another. Tilghman finally got track of him and ran him to cover, when a fight ensued. Tilghman, though shot at several times, escaped without injury and finally succeeded in killing his quarry.

"Little Dick," like his chief, Bill Doolin, had for several years made a specialty of ambushing and murdering U. S. Deputy Marshals in Oklahoma and the Indian Territory, and when the announcement of his death at the hands of Deputy Marshal Tilghman was made, there was universal rejoicing among the law-abiding citizens of that county. Space forbids that I go further into the career of William M. Tilghman at this time. It would take a volume the size of an encyclopedia to record the many daring exploits and adventures of this remarkable man. His life's history has been aptly stated by a magazine writer as almost a continuation, as far as it relates to his adventures of the frontier of Kansas in the early seventies. After a career covering a period of thirty-seven years, spent mostly on the firing line along civilization's lurid edge and after being shot at perhaps a hundred different times by the most desperate outlaws in the land, men whose unerring aim with either gun or pistol seldom failed to bring down their victims, this man Tilghman comes through it all without as much as a scratch from a bullet.

Sheriff for More Than Thirty Years

Billy Tilghman was born in Iowa in 1854, and moved to Atchinson, Kansas, in 1856, and as a boy, passed through the reign of terror known in that country in those days as the Kansas and Missouri border war, which existed for a number of years along the frontier of those two states. It was a fierce and bitter contest between the pro-slavery influences of Missouri on the one side and the abolitionists of Kansas on the other, which finally culminated in the Civil War.

At the time Alton B. Parker received the Democratic nomination in 1904, Billy Tilghman was selected by the Democratic National convention as one of the delegates to notify Mr. Parker of his nomination, and was last in New York at that time. He is still a resident of Chandler, Lincoln County, Oklahoma, and will, in all probability be elected sheriff again there this fall. He is perhaps the only frontiersman living who has been almost constantly on the job for more than a generation, who still lives on to tell the story.

CHAPTER V

WYATT EARP

Thirty-five years ago that immense stretch of territory extending from the Missouri River west to the Pacific Ocean, and from the Brazos River in Texas north to the Red

Cloud Agency in Dakota, knew no braver nor more desperate man than Wyatt Earp, the subject of this narrative.

Wyatt Earp is one of the few men I personally knew in the West in the early days, whom I regarded as absolutely destitute of physical fear. I have often remarked, and I am not alone in my conclusion, that what goes for courage in a man is generally the fear of what others will think of him— in other words, personal bravery is largely made up of self-respect, egotism, and an apprehension of the opinion of others.

Wyatt Earp's daring and apparent recklessness in time of danger is wholly characteristic; personal fear doesn't enter into the equation, and when everything is said and done, I believe he values his own opinion of himself more than that of others, and it is his own good report that he seeks to preserve. I may here cite an incident in his career that seems to me will go far toward establishing the correctness of the estimate I have made of him.

Claimed the Cards Were Crooked

He was once engaged in running a faro game in Gunnison, Colorado, in the early days of that camp; and one day while away from the gambling house, another gambler by the name of Ike Morris, who had something of a local reputation as a bad man with a gun, and who was also running a faro game in another house in the camp, went into Wyatt's game and put down a roll of bills on one of the cards and told the dealer to turn. The dealer did as he was told, and after making a turn or two, won the bet and reached out on the layout and picked up the roll of bills and deposited them in the money drawer. Morris instantly made a kick and claimed that the cards were crooked and demanded the return of his money. The dealer said that he could not give back the money, as he was only working for wages, but advised him to wait until Mr. Earp returned, and then explain matters to him, and as he was the proprietor of the game he would perhaps straighten the matter up. In a little while Wyatt returned, and Morris was on hand to tell him about the squabble with the dealer, and incidentally ask for the return of the money he had bet and lost.

Wyatt told him to wait a minute and he would speak to the dealer about it; if things were as he represented he would see what could be done about it. Wyatt stepped over to the dealer and asked him about the trouble with Morris. The dealer explained the matter, and assured Wyatt that there was nothing wrong with the cards, and that Morris had lost his money fairly and squarely. By this time the house was pretty well filled up, as it got noised about that Morris and Earp were likely to have trouble. A crowd had gathered in anticipation of seeing a little fun. Wyatt went over to where Morris was standing and stated that the dealer had admitted cheating him out of his money, and he felt very much like returning it on that account; but said Wyatt, "You are looked upon in this part of the country as a bad man, and if I was to give you back your money you would say as soon as I left, that you made me do it, and for that reason I will keep the money." Morris said no more about the matter, and after inviting Wyatt to have a cigar, returned to his house, and in a day or so left the camp.

Lost His Reputation In The Camp

There was really no reason why he should have gone away, for so far as Wyatt was concerned the incident was closed; but he perhaps felt that he had lost whatever prestige his reputation as a bad man had given him in the camp, and concluded it would be best for him to move out before some other person of lesser note than Wyatt Earp took a fall out of him. This he knew would be almost sure to happen if he remained. He did not need to be told that if he remained in town after the Earp incident got noised about, every Tom, Dick and Harry in camp would be anxious to take a kick at him, and that was perhaps the reason for his sudden departure for other fields where the fact of his punctured reputation was not so generally known.

The course pursued by Earp on this occasion was undoubtedly the proper one—in fact the only one, to preserve his reputation and self respect. It would not have been necessary for him to have killed Morris in order to have sustained his reputation, and very likely that was the very thing he had in mind at the time, for he was not one of those human tigers who delighted in shedding blood just for the fun of the thing. He never, at any time in his career, resorted to the pistol excepting in cases where such a course was absolutely necessary. Wyatt could scrap with his fist, and had often taken all the fight out of bad men, as they were called, with no other weapons than those provided by nature.

There were few men in the West who could whip Earp in a rough-and-tumble fight thirty years ago, and I suspect that he could give a tough youngster a hard tussle right now, even if he is sixty-one years of age. In all probability had Morris been known as a peaceable citizen, he would have had his money returned when he asked for it, as Wyatt never cared much for money; but being known as a man with a reputation as a gun-fighter, his only chance to get his money back lay in his ability to "do" Earp, and that was a job he did not care to tackle.

I have known Wyatt Earp since early in the seventies, and have seen him tried out under circumstances which made the test of manhood supreme. He landed in Wichita, Kansas, in 1872, being then about twenty-six years old, and weighing in the neighborhood of one hundred and sixty pounds, all of it muscle. He stood six feet in height, with light blue eyes, and a complexion bordering on the blonde. He was born at Monmouth, Illinois, of a clean strain of American breeding, and served in an Iowa regiment the last three years of the Civil War, although he was only a boy at the time. He always arrayed himself on the side of law and order, and on a great many occasions, at the risk of his life, rendered valuable service in upholding the majesty of the law in those communities in which he lived. In the spring of 1876 he was appointed Assistant City Marshall of Dodge City, Kansas, which was then the largest shipping point in the North for the immense herds of Texas cattle

that were annually driven from Texas to the northern markets. Wyatt's reputation for courage and coolness was well
known to many of the citizens of Dodge City—in fact it
was his reputation that secured for him the appointment
of Assistant City Marshall.

He was not very long on the force before one of the
aldermen of the city, presuming somewhat on the authority
his position gave him over a police officer, ordered Wyatt
one night to perform some official act that did not look
exactly right to him, and Wyatt refused point blank to obey
the order. The alderman, regarded as something as a scrap-
per himself, walked up to Wyatt and attempted to tear his
official shield from his vest front where it was pinned. When
that alderman woke up he was a greatly changed man.
Wyatt knocked him down as soon as he laid his hands on
him, and then reached down and picked him up with one
hand and slammed a few hooks and upper-cuts into his face,
dragged his limp form over to the city calaboose, and
chucked it in one of the cells, just the same as he would any
other disturber of the peace. The alderman's friends tried to
get him out on bail during the night, but Wyatt gave it out
that it was the calaboose for the alderman until the police
court opened up for business at nine o'clock the following
morning, and it was. Wyatt was never bothered any more
while he lived in Dodge City by aldermen.

While he invariably went armed, he seldom had occasion
to do any shooting in Dodge City, and only once do I recall
when he shot to kill, and that was at a drunken cowboy,
who rode up to a Variety Theater where Eddie Foy, the
now famous comedian, was playing an engagement. The
cowboy rode right by Wyatt, who was standing outside the
main entrance to the show shop, but evidently he did not
notice him, else he would not in all probability have acted
as he did.

An Incident Not On the Program

The building in which the show was being given was

one of those pine-board affairs that were in general use in frontier towns. A bullet fired from a Colt's 45 calibre pistol would go through a half-dozen such buildings, and this the cowboy knew. Whether it was Foy's act that enraged him, or whether he had been jilted by one of the chorus we never learned; at any rate he commenced bombarding the side of the building directly opposite the stage upon which Eddy Foy was at that very moment reciting that beautifully pathetic poem entitled "Kalamazoo in Michigan." The bullets tore through the side of the building, scattering pieces of the splintered pine-boards in all directions. Foy evidently thought the cowboy was after him, for he did not tarry long in the line of fire. The cowboy succeeded in firing three shots before Wyatt got his pistol in action. Wyatt missed at the first shot, which was probably due to the fact that the horse the cowboy was riding kept continually plunging around, which made it rather a hard matter to get a bead on him. His second shot, however, did the work, and the cowboy rolled off his horse and was dead by the time the crowd reached him.

Wyatt's career in and around Tombstone, Arizona, in the early days of that bustling mining camp was perhaps the most thrilling and exciting of any he ever experienced in the thirty-five years he has lived on the lurid edge of civilization. He had four brothers besides himself who waggoned it into Tombstone as soon as it was announced that gold had been discovered in the camp.

Jim was the oldest of the brothers, Virgil came next, then Wyatt, then Morgan, and Warren, who was the kid of the family. Jim started in running a saloon as soon as one was built. Virgil was holding the position of Deputy U.S. Marshal. Wyatt operated a gambling house, and Morgan rode as a Wells Fargo shot-gun messenger on the coach that ran between Tombstone and Benson, which was the nearest railroad point. Morgan's duty was to protect the Wells Fargo coach from the stage robbers with which the country at that time was infested.

Stage Robbers of San Simon Valley

The Earps and the stage robbers knew each other personally, and it was on this account that Morgan had been selected to guard the treasure the coach carried. The Wells Fargo Company believed that so long as it kept one of the Earp boys on their coach their property was safe; and it was, for no coach was ever held up in that country upon which one of the Earp boys rode as guard.

A certain band of those stage robbers who lived in the San Simon Valley, about fifty miles from Tombstone and very near the line of Old Mexico, where they invariably took refuge when hard pressed by the authorities on the American side of the line, was made up of the Clanton brothers, Ike and Billy, and the McLowry brothers, Tom and Frank. This was truly a quartette of desperate men, against whom the civil authorities of that section of the country at that time were powerless to act. Indeed, the United States troops from the surrounding posts who had been sent out to capture them dead or alive, had on more than one occasion returned to their posts after having met with both failure and disaster at the hands of the desperadoes.

Those were the men who had made up their minds to hold up and rob the Tombstone coach; but in order to do so with as little friction as possible, they must first get rid of Morgan Earp. They could as a matter of course, ambush him and shoot him dead from the coach; but that course would hardly do, as it would be sure to bring on a fight with the other members of the Earp family and their friends, of whom they had a great many. They finally concluded to try diplomacy. They sent word to Morgan to leave the employ of the Wells Fargo Express Company, as they intended to hold up the stage upon which he acted as guard, but didn't want to do it as long as the coach was in his charge. Morgan sent back word that he would not quit and that they had better not try to hold him up or there would be trouble. They then sent word to Wyatt to have him induce Morgan, if such a thing was possible, to quit his job, as they had fully determined on holding up the coach and killing Morgan if it became necessary in order to carry out their purpose.

Wyatt sent them back word that if Morgan was determined to continue riding as guard for Wells Fargo he would not interfere with him in any way, and that if they killed him he would hunt them down and kill the last one in the bunch. Just to show the desperate character of those men, they sent Virgil Earp, who was City Marshal of Tombstone at the time, word that on a certain day they would be in town prepared to give him and his brothers a battle to the death. Sure enough, on the day named Ike and Billy Clanton, and Tom and Frank McLowry rode into Tombstone and put their horses up in one of the city corrals. They were in town some little time before the Earps knew it. They never suspected for a moment that the Clantons and McLowrys had any intention of carrying out their threat when they made it. When Virgil Earp fully realized that they were in town he got very busy. He knew that it meant a fight and was not long in rustling up Wyatt and Morgan and "Doc" Holliday, the latter as desperate a man in a tight place as the West ever knew. This made the Marshal's party consist of the Marshal himself, his brothers Wyatt and Morgan, and "Doc" Holliday. Against them the two Clantons and the two McLowrys, an even thing so far as numbers were concerned. As soon as Virgil Earp got his party together, he started for the corral, where he understood the enemy was entrenched, prepared to resist to the death the anticipated attack of the Earp forces.

The Town Turned Out for the Battle

Everybody in Tombstone seemed to realize that a bloody battle was about to be fought right in the very center of town, and all those who could, hastened to find points of vantage from which the impending battle could be viewed in safety. It took the City Marshal some little time to get his men together, as both Wyatt and Holliday were still sound asleep in bed, and getting word to them and the time it took them to get up and dress themselves and get to the place Virge and Morgan were in waiting, necessarily caused some little delay. The invaders, who had been momentarily expecting an attack could not understand the cause for this delay, and finally concluded that the Earps were afraid and did not intend to attack them, at any rate while they were in the corral. This conclusion caused them to change their plan of battle. They instantly resolved that if "the mountain would not come to Mahomet—Mahomet would go to the mountain." If the Earps would not come to the corral, they would go and hunt up the Earps. Their horses were nearby, saddled, bitted and ready for instant use. Each man took his horse by the bridle-line and led him through the corral-gate to the street where they intended to mount.

But just as they reached the street, and before they had time to mount their horses, the Earp party came around the corner. Both sides were now within ten feet of each other. There were four men on a side, every one of whom had during his career been engaged in other shooting scrapes and were regarded as being the most desperate of desperate men. The horses gave the rustlers quite an advantage in the position. The Earps were in the open street, while the invaders used their horses for breastworks. Virgil Earp, as the City Marshal, ordered the Clantons and McLowrys to throw up their hands and surrender. This order they replied to with a volley from their pistols. The fight was on now. The Earps pressed in close, shooting as rapidly as they could. The fight was hardly started before it was over, and the result showed that nearly every shot fired by the Earp party went straight home to the mark.

Further Developments of the Feud

As soon as the smoke of battle cleared away sufficiently to permit of an accounting being made, it was seen that the two McLowrys and Billy Clanton were killed. They had been hit by no less than half a dozen bullets each, and died in their tracks. Morgan Earp was the only one of the Marshal's force that got hit. It was nothing more, however, than a slight flesh wound in one of his arms. Ike Clanton made his escape, but in doing so he stamped himself as a coward of the first magnitude. No sooner had the shooting commenced than he threw down his pistol and with both hands high above his head, he ran to Wyatt Earp and begged him not to kill him. Here again Wyatt showed the kind of stuff that was in him, for instead of killing Clanton as most any other man would have done under the circumstances, he told him to run away, and he did.

The Earp party were all tried for this killing, and after a preliminary examination lasting several weeks, during which more than a hundred witnesses were examined, they were all exonerated. There were at this time two other out-law bands in the country, who, when they heard of the kill-ing of the McLowry brothers and Billy Clanton, swore to wipe out the Earp family and all their friends. They had no notion, however, of giving the Earps any more battles in the open. In the future, killings would be done from am-bush, and the first one to get potted by this guerilla system of warfare was Virge Earp, the City Marshal. As he was crossing one of the most prominent corners in Tombstone one night he was fired upon by some one not then known, but who was afterwards learned to be "Curly Bill," who was concealed behind the walls of a building that was then in course of construction on one of the corners. A shotgun load-ed with buckshot was the weapon used. Most of the charge struck Virge in the left arm between the shoulder and elbow, shattering the bone in a frightful manner. One or two other shot hit him but caused no serious injury. He was soon able to be about again, but never had any use afterward of his left arm. As a matter of course the shock he sustained when the buckshot hit him caused him to fall, and the would-be assassin, thinking he had turned the trick successfullv, made his escape in the dark to the foothills. The next to get mur-dered was Morgan Earp, who was shot through a window one night while playing a game of pin-pool with a friend.

Wyatt then realized that it was only a question of time until he and all his friends would be killed in the same manner as his brother, if he remained in town. So, he organized a party consisting of himself, "Doc" Holliday, Jack Vermillion, Sherman McMasters, and Bill Johnson, and after equipping it with horses, guns and plenty of ammunition, started out on the war-path intending to hunt down and kill every one he could find who had any hand in the murder of his brother and the attempted assassination of Virge. Wyatt had in the meantime, learned that Pete Spence, Frank Stillwell, and a Mexican, by the name of Florentine, were the three who were interested in the killing of Morgan. Pete Spence had a ranch about twenty-five miles from Tombstone near the Dragoon Mountains, which was in reality nothing more than a rendezvous for cattle thieves and stage robbers.

Wyatt and his party headed straight for the Spence ranch as soon as he left Tombstone on his campaign of revenge. He found only the Mexican when he reached the ranch, and after making some inquiry as to the whereabouts of Spence, and learning that he had left early that morning for Tombstone by a different route from the one the Earps had traveled, proceeded, without further ceremony, to shoot the Mexican to pieces with buckshot. They left the greaser's body where it fell, and returned to Tombstone, where they expected to find Spence. He was there all right enough, but seemingly to anticipate what Wyatt intended doing, had gone to the sheriff, who was not on friendly terms with the Earp faction, and surrendered, having himself locked up in jail.

Of course, Wyatt had to let him go for the time being, and was getting ready to start out on another expedition when he received word from Tucson that Frank Stillwell and Ike Clanton were there. Wyatt and "Doc" Holliday immediately started for Benson, where they took the train for Tucson, which was about sixty miles farther south. Both were armed with shotguns, and just before the train came to a stop at the Tucson station, Wyatt and Holliday, from the platform of the rear coach, saw Clanton and Stillwell standing on the depot platform. They immediately jumped off and started for the depot, intending to kill them both, but they were seen coming by the quarry who had evidently been made aware of Earp's movements and were on the lookout at the station. Clanton and Stillwell started to run as soon as they saw Wyatt and Holliday approaching, Stillwell down the railroad track and Clanton towards town. Wyatt and Holliday immediately gave chase to Stillwell and succeeded after a short run in overtaking him. He threw up his hands and begged not to be killed, but it was too late. Besides, Wyatt had given instructions that no prisoners should be taken, so they riddled his body with buckshot and left it where it fell, just as they had the Mexican. Wyatt and Holliday then returned to Tombstone, thinking there might still be a chance to get a crack at Pete Spence, but the latter still clung to the jail.

Defying the Sheriff of Tombstone

Meanwhile the sheriff of Tombstone had received telegraphic instructions from the sheriff of Tucson to arrest Wyatt and Holliday as soon as they showed up, for the murder of Stillwell. When Wyatt got back to town, he hustled his men together for the purpose of going after Curly Bill, whom he believed to be the man who shot Virge from ambush. When the sheriff and his posse reached Wyatt, the latter and his crowd were about to mount their horses preparatory to going on the "Curly Bill" expedition.

"Wyatt, I want to see you," said the sheriff.

"You will see me once too often," replied Wyatt, as he bounded into the saddle. "And remember," continued Wyatt to the sheriff, "I'm going to get that hound you are protecting in jail when I come back, if I have to tear the jail down to do it."

The sheriff made no further attempt to arrest Wyatt and Holliday. The next night Wyatt killed Curly Bill at the Whetstone Spring, about thirty miles from Tombstone and just to make his word good with the sheriff, he and his party returned to town, The sheriff, however, had during his absence released Spence and told him to get across the Mexican border with as little delay as possible if he valued

his life, for the Earp gang would surely kill him if he didn't.
This ended the Earp campaign in Arizona for the time
being. Much has been written about Wyatt Earp that is the
veriest rot, and every once in a while a newspaper article
will appear in which it is alleged that some person had taken
a fall out of him, and that when he had been put to the test,
had shown the white feather. Not long ago a story was
published in different newspapers throughout the country
that some little Canadian police officer somewhere in the
Canadian Northwest had given Wyatt an awful call-down;
had, in fact, taken his pistol from him and in other ways
humiliated him. The story went like wildfire, as all such
stories do, and was printed and reprinted in all the big dailies
in the country. There was not one word of truth in it, and
the newspaper fakir who unloaded the story on the reading
public very likely got no more than ten dollars for his work.
Wyatt, to begin with, was never in the Canadian Northwest,
and therefore was never in a position where a little Canadian police officer could have taken such liberties with him as
those described by the author of the story. Take it from
me, no one has ever humiliated this man Earp, nor made
him show the white feather under any circumstances whatever. While he is now a man past sixty, there are still a great
many so-called bad men in this country who would be found,
if put to test, to be much easier game to tackle than this
same lean and lanky Earp.

Wyatt Earp, like many more of his character who lived
in the West in its early days, has excited, by his display of
great courage and nerve under trying conditions, the envy
and hatred of those small minded creatures with which the
world seems to be abundantly peopled, and whose sole de-
light in life seems to be in fly-specking the reputations of
real men. I have known him since the early seventies and
have always found him a quiet, unassuming man, not given
to brag or bluster, but at all times and under all circumstances a loyal friend and an equally dangerous enemy.

"An Oldtime Cowboy"
Drawn by Pink Simms, an oldtime cowboy, for Rose Collection, 1935.

Bat Masterson

Bat Masterson, author and newspaper man.

Luke Short

Wyatt Earp, as he appeared in 1886.

Wyatt Earp, as he appeared in 1926.

Ben Thompson, age 29 years.
Wichita, Kansas, 1872.

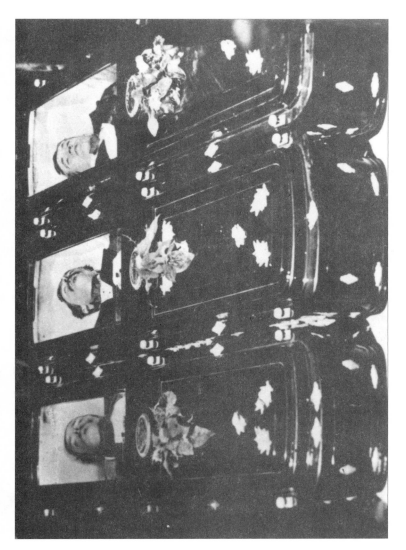

Tom and Frank McLowery, and Billy Clanton, killed in the battle at the OK Corral, Tombstone.

Ben. Thompson

who was killed March 11, 1884, with King Fisher,
in Jack Harris Theater, San Antonio, Texas.

Ben Thompson

Bill Tilghman, U.S. Marshall—an officer for fifty years.
Killed at Cromwell, Oklahoma, October 30, 1926.

J. H. (Doc) Holliday, as he appeared in the early eighties.

Dodge City, Kansas, 1877.
1—Wolf & Co., 2—Smith, Edwards & Co., 3—the old dance hall,
4—wagons loaded with buffalo hides just in from the ranges.

Dodge City, Kansas, 1878, Front Street.
The first hotel, the Dodge House, is shown in the foreground.

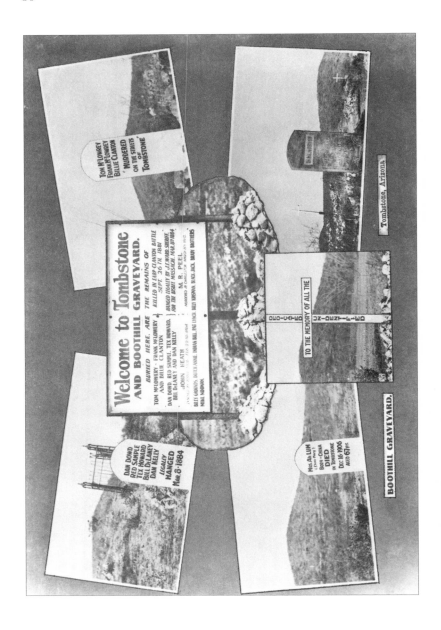

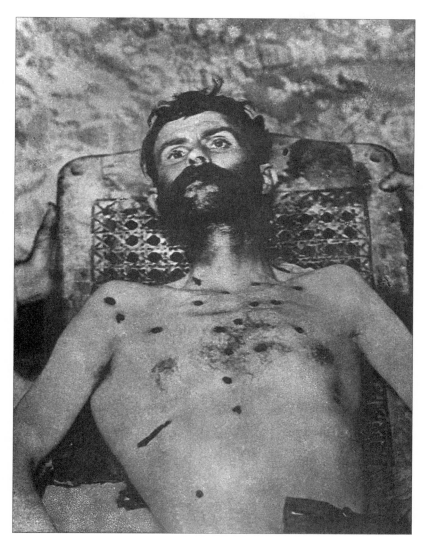

The notorious Bill Doolin, leader of the famous Doolin outlaw gang.

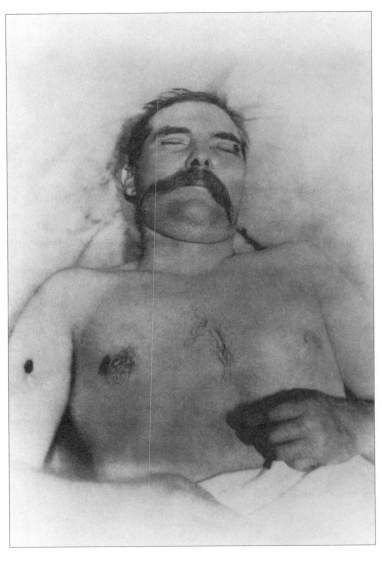

John Wesley Hardin, killed in El Paso, Texas, August 19, 1895.

John Wesley Hardin

The last photo made of Wild Bill. 1876.

Jack Harris

Billy Thompson, photo made in
Ellsworth, Kansas, 1872.

Col. Wm. Breakenridge,
in the Heldorado parade, Tombstone, Arizona.
Photo by Arizona Republic, Phoenix.

John King Fisher, when he was deputy sheriff of Uvalde County, Texas, who was killed with Ben Thompson, in the old Jack Harris theater, March 11, 1884, San Antonio, Texas.

Morgan Earp, as he appeared in 1880.

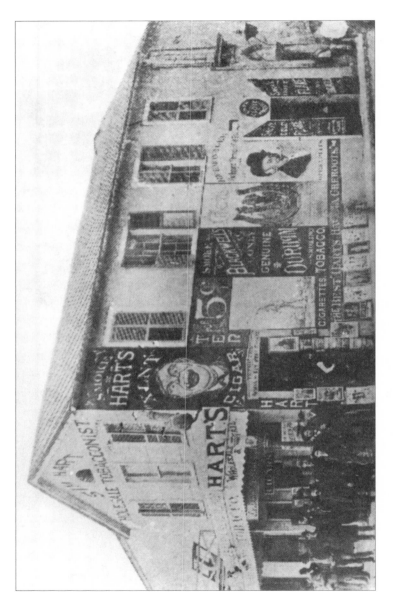

Northwest corner of Commerce and Soledad streets, 1885, site of present National Bank of Commerce, showing Sim Hart's Cigar Store. Second story occupied by "101" Gambling Rooms. Jack Harris' Famous Variety Show, was in the rear.

STATE OF TEXAS, }
COUNTY OF BEXAR

The State of Texas to any Legal Officer of said County, GREETING:

YOU ARE HEREBY COMMANDED TO SUMMON

Wm. Hitchcock, Mrs. May Martin, Geo. Ross Higgins, Benj. McEntee, L. W. Hitchcock, &c.

if to be found in your County, to be and appear on Tuesday January 9th A. D. 188 7, before our Honorable District Court for said County, now in session at the Courthouse in San Antonio, then and there to give evidence in a case therein pending, wherein THE STATE OF TEXAS is plaintiff, and Geo. Thompson

is defendant, on behalf of the State

and that they continue their attendance from day to day and term to term until duly discharged.

HEREIN FAIL NOT, but of this Writ make due return as the law directs.

WITNESS, GEORGE R. DASHIELD, District Clerk of Bexar County,

this 8th day of January A. D. 1883

Theo. Vallino

Clerk District Court Bexar County

By Daniel Maris Jr
Deputy.

[Issued same day.]

No. 2118

THE STATE OF TEXAS,
vs.

Geo. Thompson

SUBPŒNA.

Returned Term A. D. 188 ...

Filed January A. D. 188 3

Hugh Wild
Clerk District Court

By Manuel Chaves Deputy.

Came to hand January 8, 188 3

and executed the within .... by summoning the within .... to appear before said Court at the time specified.

E. P. McCall
Sheriff Bexar County

R. B. Alexander Deputy

Texas West Print, No. 3 W. Houston, San Antonio.

Virgil Earp
1887

James Earp
1881

Jim McIntyre, noted Texas Pan-handle Gunman.
Friend of Jim Courtright.

Last trip of old Modoc Stage, Tombstone, Ariz.

Old Crystal Bar, Tombstone, Arizona.

Jim Courtright, Union scout, frontier character and man slayer. Killed by Luke Short in a personal encounter in Ft. Worth, February 8, 1886.

A. H. (Shanghai) Pierce, the last and best picture ever made of him.

Tombstone, Arizona, 1955.

Present day Tombstone.

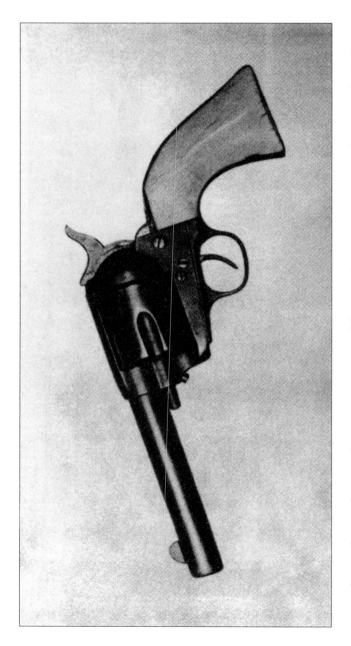

John Wesley Hardin's Single Action Army .45 Caliber Revolver, No.126680, one of two guns he had on his person, at the time he was killed by John Selman, at El Paso, Texas, August 19, 1895. It is now the property of his grand-daughter. This photo made and COPYRIGHTED by N. H. Rose, 1938.

This is a group of Dodge City, Kansas, gun-fighters, in 1870, from an old photograph taken in Kansas City, in 1871. Reading from left to right, they are, top row: W. H. Harris, Luke Short, Bat Masterson,—sitting: D. Bassett, Wyatt Earp, McNeal, and Neal Brown.

Bird's Eye View of Tombstone, Arizona, 1880.

Sheriff John Slaughter, Tombstone, Arizona.

Bill Tilghman and C. F. Celeard, Deputy U. S. Marshals,
at the opening of Cherokee Strip, Perry, Oklahoma, Sept. 1893.

Old Crystal Bar, Tombstone, Ariz.

Group of old timers in Arizona. Left to right, standing; 1—C. B. Tarbell; 2—not identified; 3—Dan Shoemaker; 4—Bill Hattick; 5—A. W. Wentworth; 6—John Montz; 7—Mike Crowley; 8—A. W. Smith; 9—W. A. King; 10—B. Hattick. Down in front: 11—J. N. McDonough; 12—Harry Draeger; 13—Cal Hafford; 14—Frank (Fatty) Ryan. (Photo furnished by Rose Tree Inn, Tombstone, Ariz.)

A Difficult Stunt.
Ed McGivern putting six shots in a tin-can, before it can fall to the ground using Smith & Wesson Double-Action Revolver.

Most widely publicized photograph of the American West.

Judge Roy Bean, the "Law West of the Pecos," holding court at the old town of Langtry, Texas, in 1900, trying a horse thief. This building was courthouse and saloon. No other peace officers in the locality at that time.

Bill Raidler, of the Bill Doolin outlaw gang.

Buildings in the present day ghosttown of old Shakespeare, near Lordsburg, NM. It was here that the "cowboys" Curly Bill, John Ringo, Jim Hughs, and their friends, came during the lull in their battles with the Earp gang of Tombstone.

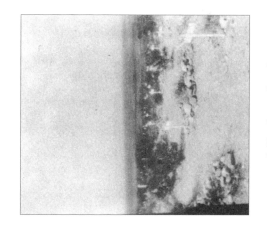

Present day Tombstone, Arizona.

Boothill, where they lay.

The Epitaph.

Jack Blake, alias Tulsa Jack, of the famous Doolin gang.